GREAT OUTDOORS COLORADO TRUST FUND

This trail head and 2400 feet of trail were designed and constructed with a matching grant from the Great Outdoors Colorado Trust Fund. This is your lottery funds at work.

John Fielder's Guide to

Colorado's
Great Outdoors

Lottery-Funded Parks, Trails, Wildlife Areas & Open Spaces

Photography and Text by John Fielder
Published in Cooperation with the Great Outdoors Colorado Trust Fund

JOHN FIELDER PUBLISHING

Silverthorne, Colorado

ISBN: 978-0-9860004-3-0

GRAPHIC DESIGNER: Rebecca Finkel, F + P Graphic Design

EDITOR: Deb Olson

PUBLISHED BY:
John Fielder Publishing
P.O. Box 26890
Silverthorne, Colorado 80497

FRONTISPIECE PHOTOGRAPHS:

Coal Creek Trail, Boulder County

Cherry Creek State Park,
Arapahoe County

Lawson Hill Underpass, Telluride,
San Miguel County

TITLE PAGE AND PAGE 8:
Medano-Zapata Ranch, Alamosa
County

FRONT COVER: Spruce
Mountain Open Space,
Douglas County

For more information about books and calendars published by John Fielder and John Fielder Publishing, please contact your local bookstore, web retailer, John Fielder's Colorado Gallery (303-744-7979), or visit **johnfielder.com**. Book resellers please contact Books West distributors at **bookswest.net**.

Printed in U.S.A.

Contents

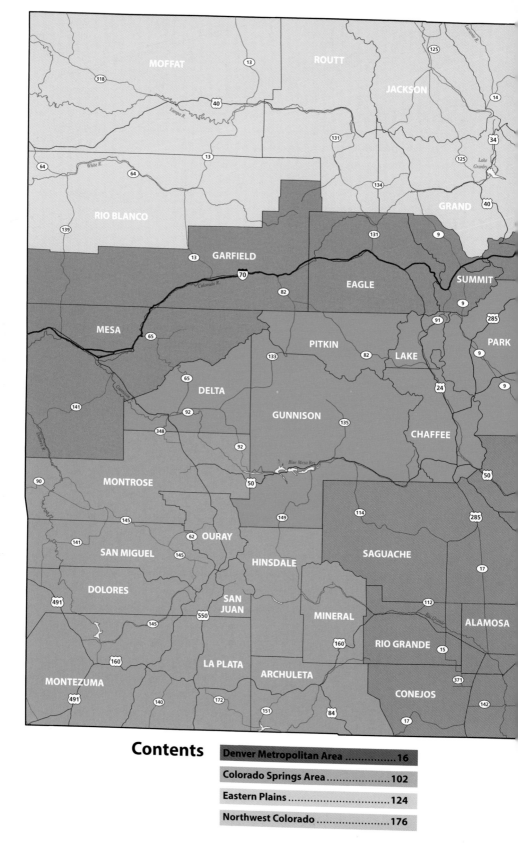

Contents

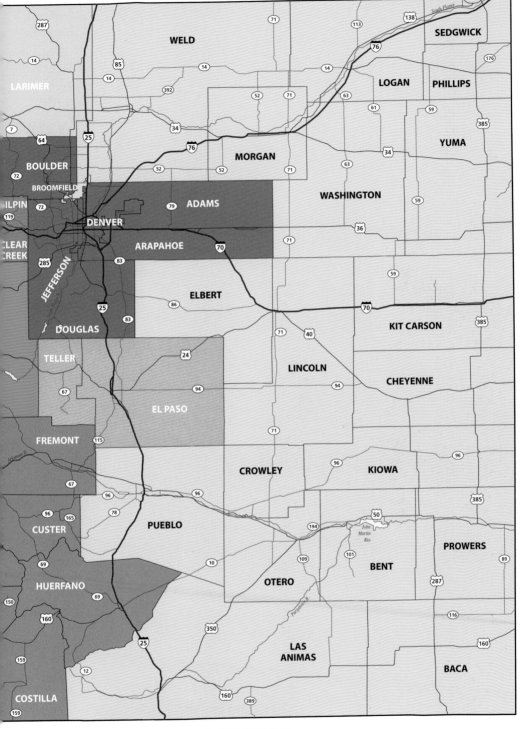

Introduction

This guide to Colorado's parks, trails, open spaces, and wildlife areas celebrates the 20th anniversary of the creation of Great Outdoors Colorado (GOCO) in 1992, and features many of the places in which GOCO has invested. It is the companion publication to *Colorado's Great Outdoors, Celebrating 20 Years of Lottery-Funded Lands,* a large format book featuring photographs of some of the most beautiful lands preserved with the help of GOCO funds, from public county open space to private working ranches.

For your convenience, this guidebook is divided into eight geographic regions, subdivided by counties (all 64 of them), and organized by cities and towns within those counties. The book includes a state map and eight regional maps, which are intended only to delineate counties, not help you find specific sites. I recommend using the very comprehensive *DeLorme's Colorado Atlas & Gazetteer* to find the Colorado communities listed in this book, as well as the network of highways and byways needed to reach them. The description of each Colorado outdoor resource contains driving directions, and sometimes an address. Websites are almost always included as well, in the event you want more information.

The Origin of Great Outdoors Colorado

To understand the origins of the Great Outdoors Colorado Trust Fund, you first must understand the history of Colorado Lottery proceeds. When Coloradans voted to create a lottery in 1980, the issue put to voters was: "An amendment to Section 2 of Article XVIII of the Constitution of the State of Colorado, authorizing the establishment of a state-supervised lottery with the net proceeds—unless otherwise authorized by statute—allocated to the conservation trust fund of the state for distribution to municipalities and counties for park, recreation, and open space purposes." This measure passed with 59.8% of voters in favor. The Colorado Lottery was implemented on July 1, 1982 when the General Assembly passed Senate Bill 119. The distribution formula in that bill was different than the ballot language. It directed that 40 percent of net proceeds be allocated to the Conservation Trust Fund to support local parks, recreation, and open space projects; 10 percent be allocated to state parks and outdoor recreation programs; and the remaining net proceeds be allocated to state capital construction projects.

Fast forward to 1990: Ken Salazar, the newly-appointed executive director of the Colorado Department of Natural Resources, beseeched Governor Roy Romer to create a committee that would explore ways to invest in Colorado's natural heritage. While considering the inconsistency between the Lottery proceeds distribution formula and the intent of voters, the committee of interested citizens also looked at many revenue sources that could benefit Colorado's outdoor resources, including sales and property taxes. The committee ultimately recommended to Governor Romer that the 50 percent of Lottery proceeds allocated for capital construction projects be redirected to benefit local parks, recreation, and open space projects, as Coloradans had originally intended.

The Governor agreed, but the General Assembly refused to refer a measure to the people, so an effort was launched to gather enough signatures to place a citizens' initiative on the 1992 ballot. The initiative passed handily and gave the former state capital construction money to the Great Outdoors Colorado Trust Fund, with the stipulation that it be capped at $35 million per year, adjusted annually for the cost of living index, and that any leftover money be returned to the state's general fund (this has subsequently changed so that leftover money now goes to the school capital construction fund). The ballot measure also reaffirmed that 40 percent of Lottery proceeds go to the Conservation Trust Fund and 10 percent to Colorado's state parks.

About Great Outdoors Colorado
The Mission
Great Outdoors Colorado's mission is to help preserve, protect, enhance, and manage the state's wildlife, park, river, trail, and open space heritage.

The Colorado Constitution requires GOCO to allocate its proceeds to four areas in substantially equal portions over time:

- "Investments in the wildlife resources of Colorado through the Colorado Division of Wildlife (as of 2011, the Colorado Division of Parks and Wildlife), including the protection and restoration of crucial wildlife habitats, appropriate programs for maintaining Colorado's diverse wildlife heritage, wildlife watching, and educational programs about wildlife and wildlife environment."

- "Investments in the outdoor recreation resources of Colorado through the Colorado Division of Parks and Outdoor Recreation (as of 2011, the Colorado Division of Parks and Wildlife), including the State Parks system, trails, public information and environmental education resources, and water for recreational facilities."

- "Competitive grants to the Colorado Division of Parks and Wildlife, and to counties, municipalities, or other political subdivisions of the state, or non-profit land conservation organizations, to identify, acquire, and manage open space and natural areas of statewide significance."

- "Competitive matching grants to local governments or other entities which are eligible for distributions from the Conservation Trust Fund, to acquire, develop, or manage open lands and parks."

From these four funding areas, GOCO has developed a variety of grant programs.

Accomplishments

Since awarding its first grants in 1994 through 2011, GOCO has committed more than $715 million for nearly 3,500 projects in all 64 counties throughout the state. GOCO dollars have helped:

- protect more than 837,000 acres of open space in perpetuity, including land along river corridors and in mountain valleys; land for wildlife habitat; agricultural land; land in the heart of cities; land that separates communities; and land that buffers state and local parks from encroaching development.

- create or enhance 1,172 community park and outdoor recreation areas, including skate parks, ball fields, and playgrounds.

- assist the Colorado Division of Parks and Wildlife in acquiring and enhancing wildlife habitat; improving species' status to delist or prevent them from being listed under the federal Threatened and Endangered Species Program; providing wildlife viewing opportunities; enhancing facilities at existing state parks; buying land and providing facilities at new state parks; acquiring buffers to protect parks from encroaching development; and providing youth education.

- build or restore nearly 720 miles of trail.

- enable thousands of teenagers and young adults to participate in the Colorado Youth Corps Association.

- offer consistent, current and complete information about the status and trends of open space lands throughout Colorado via the state's first inventory of open space. The inventory provides detailed maps with comprehensive attributes listed for each parcel of land.

The GOCO Amendment created a diverse Board to oversee distribution of funds and represent all corners of the state. It consists of two members from each congressional district, two representatives designated by the Division of Parks and Wildlife Commission, and the Executive Director of the Department of Natural Resources. GOCO Board members are appointed by the Governor, subject to the consent of the Senate, for terms of four years. At least two members must reside west of the Continental Divide, and at least one must represent agricultural interests.

GOCO's staff and outside experts evaluate each grant application. The staff then submits recommendations to the GOCO Board, which makes all final funding decisions.

GOCO continues to keep administrative expenses low: Its operating expenses, Board expenses, and capital investments combined remain less than 4 percent of total revenues received.

GOCO cannot and does not buy land, but makes grants to local governments, land trusts, and the Colorado Division of Parks and Wildlife. These entities either purchase land outright or work with landowners to place conservation easements on their properties.

When landowners agree to place a conservation easement on their property, they sell the development rights to their land, not the land itself. This provides landowners with a stream of income and enables them to continue agricultural production while preventing the land from ever being developed. The land remains privately-owned and on the state's tax rolls. Conservation easements placed on agricultural land protect important wildlife habitat and scenic views.

GOCO and Colorado Children

GOCO's investments in Colorado are visible in communities throughout the state. However, the organization's soundest investment—and one that offers the greatest return—just may be its continued investment in Colorado's children and young adults. Statewide, school-based and education-related projects have garnered nearly $20 million in GOCO/Lottery funds over the years. GOCO-funded projects range from vital school facilities and resources like playgrounds, outdoor classrooms, running tracks, ball fields, and tennis courts to educational programming offered through the Division of Parks and Wildlife. GOCO-funded environmental education programs at various state parks have been recognized for excellence by the Colorado Alliance for Environmental Education.

GOCO was instrumental in starting the Colorado Youth Corps Association (CYCA), which creates opportunities for young people to participate in high-quality youth corps statewide. Participants construct trails, remove weeds, and help remove beetle kill while receiving environmental education and developing an appreciation for Colorado's outdoors. With approximately 1,800 annual participants, CYCA received $1 million from GOCO in 2011 to continue its work in state parks and on wildlife habitat, and expand work for local governments and land trusts.

While GOCO has long recognized the importance of connecting youth and families with the outdoors, this was reaffirmed when the GOCO Board adopted a revised strategic plan in April 2010. The result of an extensive process that included 14 public meetings held throughout the state, GOCO's Strategic Plan identifies priorities and initiatives for the GOCO Board, and guides GOCO's grant-making and investments for the next five to 10 years—all within the confines of the GOCO Amendment to the Constitution. "Youth, Families and the Outdoors" was among the top three funding priorities identified in the Strategic Plan, with the specific goal of increasing participation by youth and families in all areas of GOCO's mission.

To help accomplish this, GOCO is currently leading efforts to identify partnerships and available funding sources for providing accessible outdoor recreation for youth and families, as well as environmental education, stewardship training, and youth employment opportunities on public lands. GOCO recently awarded funds to Larimer County for a pilot project that will analyze the ties youth and families in the area have to the natural environment. The county will work with various stakeholders to explore existing nature programming and how families use it, available outdoor spaces and facilities, and the barriers to getting Larimer County youth and families connected to nature. The county will then map these gaps to create a visual model for future planning.

GOCO is taking its commitment to youth and families to the next level by using the Larimer County pilot as a template for similar studies across Colorado. Identifying statewide gaps in outdoor resources and programming for children and families will enable GOCO to invest strategically and ensure that everyone has access to Colorado's great outdoors regardless of how and where they live.

Moving Forward

Colorado's record of protecting its natural resources and promoting recreational opportunities for residents and visitors is impressive. In the 1960s and 1970s, foresighted citizens recognized the extraordinary quality of life offered by Colorado's plains, mountains, and rivers—and their appeal to people from around the world. The City and County of Denver—through the creation of its park system—and the City of Boulder, Boulder County, and Jefferson County were pioneers, not just in Colorado but nationally, in dedicating funding to protect open space, create parks, and build trails for its residents. The birth of GOCO accelerated this tradition by funding and bolstering the plans of these and so many other counties, cities, and towns, many of which have also voted to dedicate local resources to the outdoors. And, Colorado is the only state in the nation that commits virtually all of its lottery profits to protecting its natural heritage.

There were 2.2 million Colorado residents when I arrived here in 1969. By 1980, there were 2.9 million of us, and by 1990, 3.3 million people had discovered our wonderful state. These numbers seemed not to impose on our opportunity to enjoy solitude. Then the floodgates opened. One million people moved here in the decade of the 1990s, and another 700,000 after that. As of the publication of this book, there are about five million Colorado residents, most of whom use our local parks, trails, wildlife areas, state parks, and county open spaces. GOCO's birth in 1992 couldn't have been more timely. Will people stop moving to Colorado? Of course not. In the future, we could easily gain another 700,000 residents per decade, which would make eight million of us by 2050. These numbers will arguably stress the capacity of our parks and trails, and compromise the quality of the experience. Therefore, we must continue to invest in Colorado's natural heritage if we are to preserve our unique quality of life.

For most of my career, I have photographed Colorado's public lands. I have spent the last four years of my life photographing municipal and county open space, and privately-owned working ranches. At the same time, I have learned about ecology and the relationship of all living things, including us humans, with the natural environment. The integrity of biodiversity increases proportionally with the size of the land mass protected. Connecting private lands contiguously to public lands simultaneously enhances our outdoor opportunities and preserves nature. GOCO facilitates this process.

When one studies societies that survive over time and those that do not, it's clear that those that protect their forests, water supplies, and, in general, the natural environment, last the longest. They also have the most robust and sustainable economies. By investing in the outdoors, Colorado guarantees itself a steady stream of well-educated residents, relatively high-paying jobs, and billions of dollars in annual tourism revenues. Costs like medical care go down, too. People who play outdoors are healthier physically and psychologically. In nature, we refer to creatures that depend upon one another, that gain a mutual benefit from one another, as symbiotic. It is clear that in Colorado our economy and our ecology are symbiotic. It is my hope that the work of Great Outdoors Colorado will never end.

JOHN FIELDER
Nature Photographer, GOCO Board Member 1993–2000

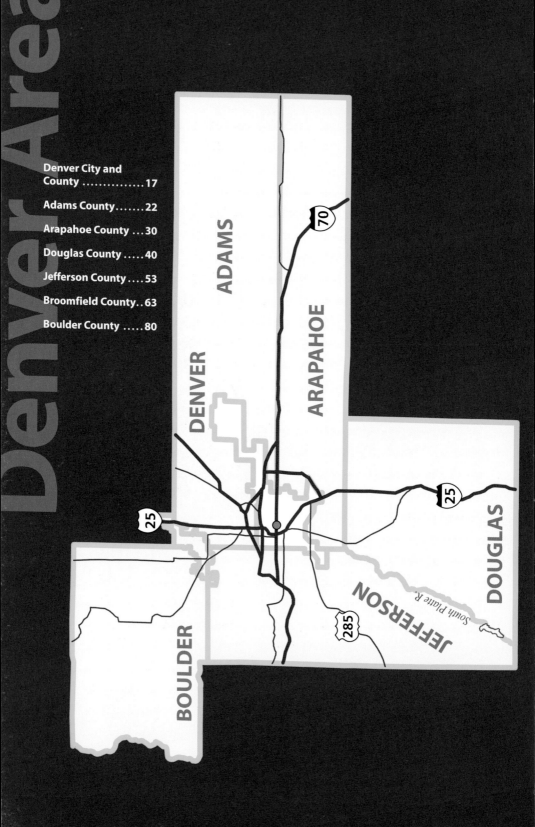

Denver Area

ADAMS

DENVER

ARAPAHOE

70

25

25

BOULDER

JEFFERSON

285

South Platte R.

DOUGLAS

The South Platte River flows from the Rocky Mountain foothills, through Denver, to the Great Plains. Like so many urban river corridors, the South Platte and its surrounding area was once sorely neglected. Working together, the Greenway Foundation, the City and County of Denver, and many other partners have created 17 riverside parks, numerous whitewater boat chutes, and a nationally-recognized urban trail system collectively known as the **South Platte River Greenway. Commons Park** and **Confluence Park,** where Cherry

Creek and the South Platte meet, are examples of this success. Maps for Denver parks, Denver hike and bike tours, and urban waterway trails are available at *www.denvergov.org./parks*

The mission of the Greenway Foundation is to advance the South Platte River and its surrounding tributaries as a unique environmental, recreational, cultural, scientific, and historical amenity that links Denver's past and future. This mission is and will be accom-

Commons Park

plished by creating ongoing environmental and riparian enhancements; holding property, when needed, in conservation easements; using the river as an outdoor and historical learning resource; hosting free cultural events promoting the relationship between the river and music, art and theatre; providing youth employment opportunities; and promoting good stewardship through hands-on educational programs. The South Platte and its tributaries are supported through the Greenway Preservation Trust. The Greenway Foundation also oversees SPREE (South Platte River Environmental Education), a youth program with a goal of

developing positive relationships between the river and students through school excursions, week-end events, summer camps, and an at-home curriculum. The foundation hosts family-friendly events each summer, including its free summer concert series. For information about these programs and cultural events, visit *www.greenwayfoundation.org.*

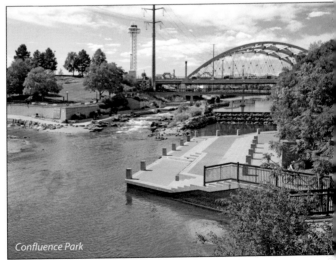

Confluence Park

The **Downtown Children's Playground** is located in the heart of Lower Downtown, aka LoDo. Features include playground equipment, colored concrete and rubberized surfacing, landscaping, furniture, and an informal sand play area. It is a favorite of city dwellers since it's right in the middle of the the Central Platte Valley near the Pepsi Center, Elitch Gardens, and the Museum of Contemporary Art Denver. Both little kids and big kids can enjoy play areas at this park located at Wewatta Street and Speer Boulevard. *www.kidsplayparks.com*

The **Mile High Loop** in Denver's City Park follows a full 5k (3.1 mile) route. The trail tracks along the city's 5,280-foot contour line, so exercisers are guaranteed a mile-high workout. You can join the trail in many locations, including just behind the Graham Bible House near the 21st & York gate, cutting between Ferril Lake and the Denver Museum of Nature & Science (where you can catch one of the best views in the city),

and running parallel to the roadway along the south side of the park. Made of crusher-fine material, the trail is pleasant and comfortable for both walkers and runners. *www.cityparkalliance.org*

Bluff Lake Nature Center occupies 123 acres adjacent to Sand Creek, which is located on the eastern edge of the Stapleton development. In the month of October, the deciduous trees are a photographer's dream, and I've made some pretty fine reflection photos here, too! A variety of native habitats include a seasonal lake, wetlands, short-grass prairie, a riparian zone, and wetland woodland. Thanks to its 60-year history as an airport buffer, Bluff Lake has become an urban wildlife refuge for waterfowl, shorebirds, raptors, songbirds, deer, fox, beaver, reptiles, amphibians, and other wildlife that visit or live at the site.

Much more than a home for plants and animals, Bluff Lake Nature Center is an oasis in the city where people can view wildlife, appreciate the sights, and enjoy the sounds of nature. Bluff Lake is also an outdoor classroom for thousands of students each year, with instructors who encourage both children and adults to have an interest in natural science and stewardship through curiosity, observation, activity, and a sense of wonder. This unique place literally brings curricula to life allowing kids who seldom experience nature to see, hear, smell, and touch their

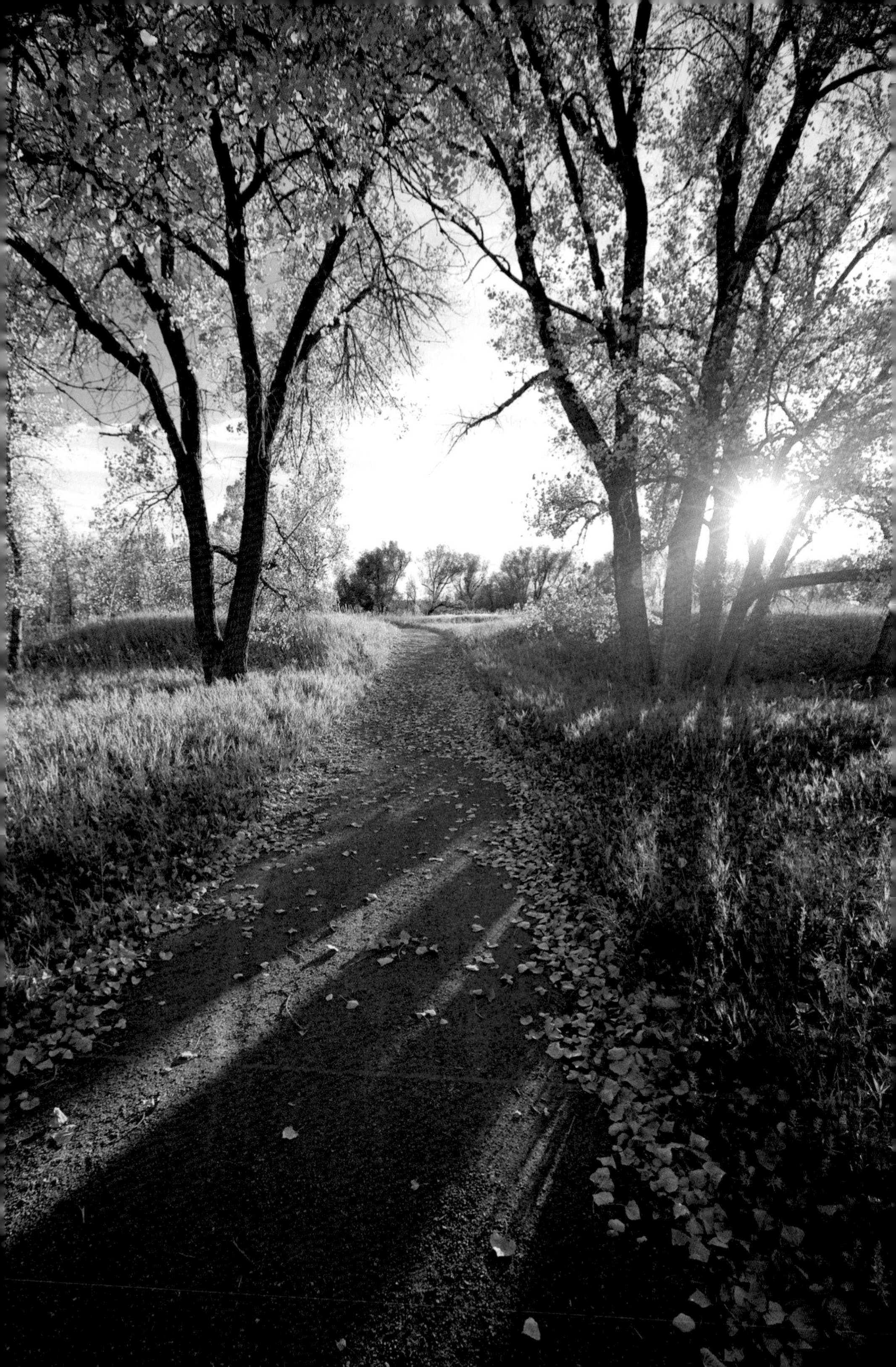

Bluff Lake Nature Center and Sand Creek Regional Greenway

lessons. Open sunrise to sunset every day, the park is protected for wildlife inhabitants, as well as for neighboring and visiting humans. Trails are for walking and jogging only; no bikes or pets allowed. Exit I-70 at Havana Street and turn south at the light off of the exit ramp. Go through the four-way stop at Smith Road and through the next light at Martin Luther King Boulevard. Turn east at the next light onto 29th Drive. Go through the light at Iola Street and follow the road as it curves to the right. The entrance to Bluff Lake is another one-half mile on the north side of the road. *www.blufflakenaturecenter.org*

Bluff Lake sits next to the **Sand Creek Regional Greenway,** a nearly 14-mile public greenway connecting the High Line Canal at Tower Road and Colfax Avenue in Aurora with the South Platte River Greenway in Commerce City. This beautiful waterway is a great place to ride your bike or take your dog. Completing a loop of 50 miles of off-street urban trails in the Northeast Denver metropolitan area, the soft-surface Sand Creek Regional Greenway trail is another jewel in the necklace of trails that has made the Denver metro area a national model for developing a linked regional trail system. With no irrigated or maintained landscapes—only native plants and grasses—it's a "Wilderness in the City." *www.sandcreekgreenway.org*

The Urban Farm serves approximately 3,000 children a year, and is home to more than 250 farm animals. The farm's 23 acres features a 20,000-square-foot indoor teaching barn, a 20,000-square-foot children's garden with a greenhouse, 24 horse paddocks, many small livestock enclosures, and a 5,000-square-foot education and office building adjacent to the farm site. The Urban Farm's purpose is to improve the lives of children living in high risk, urbanized neighborhoods by helping to foster a sense of positive self-regard and self-reliance, a strong work ethic, and hope. An underlying value of the farm is that urban children, youth, and their families will be exposed to the positive values of farm life: respect for the environment, appreciation for animals and plants, team spirit, and the satisfaction of hard work leading to a job well done. Visit it on a trip to Bluff Lake. From I-70, exit south on Havana to Smith Road. Hang a right and it's one-quarter mile on the left at 10200 Smith Road. *www.theurbanfarm.org*

Gates Tennis Center was awarded the United States Tennis Association Outstanding Large Public Facility for 2008. The public center is "pay as you play" with no residency requirements, and courtesy reservations are allowed on a day-ahead basis. Gates Tennis Center offers one of the largest ladders in the country at the following levels: Men (5.0, 4.5, 4.0, 3.5, 3.0); Women (4.5, 4.0, 3.5, 3.0, 2.5). The computerized ladder offers print-outs with names, phones, and play times available for those desiring competition within

their own level. (A small fee to participate on the ladder is required.) I spent many hours on these courts in my tennis-playing days. East of the Cherry Creek Shopping Center on East 1st Avenue, head south on Steele Street to Bayaud Avenue. You'll see the courts on the left at Adams Street and Bayaud. *www.gatestenniscenter.info*

The natural areas at **Parkfield Lake Park** include running and walking trails around a beautiful lake. New phases of development are transforming the site into a regional park with casual use areas and facilities for structured sports and events. Located at Chambers Road & 53rd Avenue in Northeast Denver. *www.denvergov.org/parks*

While it might seem like an adventure to bushwhack your way through the waist-and shoulder-high native prairie grasses at **Camp Rollandet Natural Area,** resist the temptation to do so. Staying on designated trails preserves wildlife habitat and plant biodiversity. Located between 51st and 52nd Avenues, and Sheridan Boulevard and Benton Street

in the Inspiration Point Neighborhood, this seven-acre plot of natural habitat features an enclave of upland prairie open space and wooded areas. A shrubby ravine serves as natural habitat and a corridor for birds and mammals, including fox, deer, rabbits, raccoons, and coyote. Visit in spring and summer to see bursts of blooming wild flowers in the tall grasses. The City and County of Denver purchased this historic property from the Camp Fire Girls USA. Outward Bound Denver now makes its administrative home at Camp Rollandet, providing onsite educational programming for the urban community. *www.denvergov.org/parks*

Parkfield Lake Park

Adams County

Running through Adams County, the South Platte River Corridor is the largest and most ecologically diverse river corridor in the greater metro area. Along with Barr Lake and the Rocky Mountain Arsenal National Wildlife Refuge, the South Platte River Corridor provides significant wildlife habitat, water, food, shelter, and movement corridors for 95 percent of the area's wildlife.

Aurora

Aurora City Park, located at Dayton Street and 16th Avenue, features lovely trees and a new pocket-sized skate park that was voted "Best New Skate Park" by *Westword* magazine in its 2011 Best of Denver issue. Designed by experts in Seattle, the skate park attracts skaters throughout the metro area. *www.auroragov.org*

Commerce City

See **Sand Creek Regional Greenway** on page 20. *www.sandcreekgreenway.org.* Also see **Bluff Lake Nature Center**, page 18.

Prairie Gateway Open Space and Loop Trail is a beautiful 190-acre open space northeast of the Commerce City Civic Center. Trailhead, parking, and amenities are at 64th Avenue and Quebec Street. *www.c3gov.com*

Prairie Gateway Open Space and Loop Trail

Thornton

Grandview Ponds is a pretty little park with several ponds. Stocked by the Colorado Division of Parks and Wildlife, the ponds are home to largemouth bass, crappie, carp, catfish, trout, and more, so bring your fish-

ing pole. The park includes a fishing pier for anglers using wheelchairs. Head east on 104th Avenue from Colorado Boulevard. The ponds and parking are on your right. *www.cityofthornton.net*

Thornton Community Park and Swimming Pool is located at 2525 East 94th Drive. From I-25 north, take the Thornton Parkway exit east to York Street. The park is on the right. *www.cityofthornton.net*

Grandview Ponds

Brighton

At **Barr Lake State Park,** an activity exists for nearly every type of outdoors person—from the fishing enthusiast and boater to the naturalist. Hikers, horseback riders, and bicyclists of all ages and abilities enjoy the level 8.8-mile, multi-use trail that circles the lake, passing by several wildlife viewing stations and the park's wildlife refuge. Located a short drive northeast of the Denver area, Barr Lake State Park offers the nature enthusiast a remarkable opportunity to observe all types of wildlife, including coyote, deer, and dramatic birds such as white pelicans, great blue herons, cormorants, egrets, and hawks. More than 350 species of migratory and resident birds have been seen in the park. Numerous bald eagles

winter at Barr Lake, and one pair stays to nest and raise its young every year. The southwest side of the lake is home to a bustling rookery with more than 200 nests. Visit Barr Lake's Nature Center to view displays about the park's wildlife, and get your questions answered by a naturalist.

Fishing enthusiasts and boaters, including kayakers and canoeists, appreciate the lake's calm waters: Powerboats are limited to electric trolling or gasoline motors of 10 horsepower or less. Channel catfish, small and large-mouth bass, rainbow trout, walleye, bluegill, wiper, and tiger muskie are among the species that inhabit Barr Lake. Take I-76 northeast to the Bromley Lane exit. Go east to Picadilly Road and south to the park entrance. *www.parks.state.co.us*

Barr Lake State Park

Brighton Outdoor Family Aquatic Center is located at 1852 East Bromley Lane. From Highway 85, head east on 152nd Avenue/Bromley Lane. The center will be on your right, one-half mile after Chambers Road. *www.brightonco.gov*

Rocky Mountain Bird Observatory, based at Barr Lake, conserves birds and their habitats through science, education, and stewardship in the Rocky Mountains, Great Plains and Mexico. The observatory's bird monitoring programs serve as "early warning" systems to identify trends in populations, which allows interested citizens and land managers to intervene with conservation practices that support species' long-term viability. The stewardship effort builds partnerships with private landowners to find win-win solutions for wildlife and agriculture. Providing hands-on learning experiences with birds both outdoors and in the classroom, the observatory's education programs instill a conservation ethic and an appreciation for wildlife, their habitats, and the environment. Each year, thousands of students of all ages are introduced to nature, birds and other wildlife through classroom experiences, field excursions, and camps. The observatory restored its headquarters in the Old Stone House at Barr Lake State Park, and in 2011 created an Environmental Learning Center with nature trails, bilingual interpretation of surrounding habitat, and demonstration native-plant gardens to showcase how a healthy home for birds is a healthy home for all of us. After exiting I-76 onto Bromley Lane to get to the park, take an immediate right after the railroad tracks onto Lark Bunting Lane. Drive to the end. *www.rmbo.org*

The 124-acre **Elaine T. Valente Open Space** features three lakes, access to the South Platte River Trail, wildlife viewing, and 2.1 miles of trails (both ADA-accessible and natural surface). Two wheelchair-accessible fishing piers are also on site. With the South Platte River running through the eastern portion of the park, the Elaine T. Valente Open Space protects wetlands, riparian habitat, wildlife movement corridors, and significant natural and scenic areas. It also provides natural flood management for the county. Exit I-76 onto Brighton Road, and turn west at East 104th Avenue. After crossing the river, the park is a little over a mile on your right. *www.co.adams.co.us*

Many ADA-accessible amenities can be found at **Kenneth Mitchell Park & Open Space,** including a paved trail, playground, grill, shelters, picnic tables, restrooms, benches, basketball courts, and an open play area. Several trees enhance the fine scenic view. Head north on Highway 85 and exit west onto Bromley Lane/East 152nd Avenue. Cross Platte River Boulevard and take the second street on your right, Kinglet Court, to the park. *www.brightonco.gov*

Brian Aragon Skate Park features smooth concrete, plenty of room, and a nice layout and design. Lights are on until 10 p.m. From I-76, take East 152nd Avenue west. Then go south on Judicial Center Parkway. *www.brightonco.gov*

Elaine T. Valente Open Space

Northglenn

Croke Reservoir Nature Area is a beautiful open space managed by the City to sustain wildlife, aquatic habitat, and plants. Big cottonwood trees around the lake make excellent photo subjects. Dogs are permitted on the trail just outside the nature area, along both Huron Street and Naiad Drive, but not inside the fenced area. From I-25, go west on 104th Avenue to Huron Street. Go right on Huron to the next left, Naiad Drive, which leads to Danahy Park and access to Croke. *www.northglenn.org*

Northglenn Skate Park

Northglenn Skate Park lies in the E.B. Rains, Jr. Memorial Park, just southwest of the basketball court. From I-25, take the 120th Avenue exit east to the first right, Grant Street/ Community Center Drive. Go south to the park. *www.northglenn.org*

Westminster

The crown jewel of Westminster's off-road trail system, the **Big Dry Creek Trail** is located on more than 930 acres of Westminster open space and 200 acres of parkland along the creek. The trail meanders nearly 12 miles from

Croke Reservoir Nature Area

Standley Lake Regional Park to I-25, crossing under most streets via underpasses. Designated a National Recreation Trail in 2003, the Big Dry Creek Trail is used by walkers, joggers, bicyclists, equestrians, rollerbladers, bird watchers, wildlife enthusiasts, and commuters. Abundant wildlife and native vegetation thrive along the trail corridor, bringing tranquility to this otherwise urban center. This regional trail currently connects to Thornton and ultimately will provide additional connections to the South Platte River Corridor and the communities of Broomfield and Northglenn. Maps available at *www.cityofwestminster.us.*

Arapahoe County
Aurora

The **Plains Conservation Center** is an environmental education facility totaling approximately 10,100 acres and consisting of two sites—one in Aurora and one along West Bijou Creek south of Strasburg. The center's mission is to preserve a remnant of the eastern Colorado high plains, educate the public about its natural and cultural heritage, and foster sound conservation and environmental ethics.

The Aurora site boasts five miles of hiking trails, a replica Cheyenne-style tipi encampment, and the historic Wells Crossing farm.

Programming at the site shows how people have adapted to the prairie over time. The Cheyenne Camp of tipis furnished with replicated artifacts offers visitors a glimpse into the Cheyenne way of life in the 1830s. Well Crossing, consisting of two sod homesteads, a one-room schoolhouse, a blacksmith shop, and animal sheds, gives visitors a glimpse of life in the 1880s. The heirloom garden, oxen and other heritage livestock contrast with today's commercialized food supply and reliance on fossil fuels.

The West Bijou site features breathtaking vistas, wide-open spaces, flowing streams, and

Plains Conservation Center

craggy ravines. Straddling Arapahoe and Elbert counties, this 7,794 acre-area has no public roads or other development and is bisected by West Bijou Creek. The vast size of the site allows the dynamic prairie ecosystem to thrive.

The 1,100-acre Aurora site is located at 21901 East Hampden Avenue. From E-470, take the Jewell Avenue Exit east to Gun Club Road and turn south. At East Hampden Avenue, turn west and go one mile to the gate on the north side of the road. The center is open Monday through Saturday.

The West Bijou site is located near the Arapahoe County/Elbert County line along West Bijou Creek, south of Strasburg. Currently, no facilities exist at this site, and center staff must escort all visitors for safety and security reasons. Check the website for information about when the site is open to the public (usually in late spring/early summer and in the fall). *www.plainsconservationcenter.org*

Jewell Wetlands in Aurora has been called one of the best examples of a wetlands environment in the metro area. This 50-acre wooded sanctuary within an urban landscape provides refuge for owls, hawks, and foxes, and wetland habitat for mature cottonwood groves and cattails. A garden to attract butterflies to the area was recently planted. Accessible crusher fine trails loop around the site, and boardwalks lead to an observation deck overlooking the vast wetlands. You'll find the wetlands at the northwest corner of Potomac and Jewell Avenue (just east of Utah Park), with a small parking area on the Jewell Avenue side of the property. *www.auroragov.org*

Spring Creek Park is a lovely open space that will eventually feature several athletic fields, trails, new wetlands, and a large pavilion/ shelter with seasonal restrooms. The park is located on South Himalaya Street between East Hampden Avenue and East Quincy Avenue. *www.aprd.org*

Jewell Wetlands

Red-tailed Hawk Park features an outdoor water sprayground, expansive playgrounds, six competition-size bocce ball courts, a sand volleyball area, six horseshoe pits, shaded shelters, vault restrooms, and connections to the regional Piney Creek Trail. It's located at 23701 East Hinsdale Way in Southeast Aurora at the intersection of South Aurora Parkway and East Hinsdale Way. *www.auroragov.org*

Glendale

The Park at Infinity Park is now Glendale's largest public park. A beautiful and extremely green open space, it's located immediately south of The Stadium at Infinity Park and the City of Glendale's municipal campus. Amenities include walking/jogging paths, public lawns, picnic tables, and barbecue grills as well as a park pavilion and a multi-purpose sports field. The Park at Infinity Park is located on the southwest corner of East Tennessee Avenue and South Cherry Street. *www.infinityparkeventcenter.com*

Centennial
Cherry Creek Complex

For scenery and lots of outdoor activities, the Cherry Creek corridor located in the Southeast Denver metro area rivals the South Platte River corridor in Denver's Southwest region. Just as Chatfield State Park is the hub for South Platte River activities, **Cherry Creek State Park** offers ample recreational opportunities in the Cherry Creek area. Anchored around an 880-surface acre reservoir, the park features a natural prairie environment of gentle, rolling hills and complete outdoor recreation facilities to accommodate camping, picnicking, and various group events. Visitors can participate in both traditional park activities or those considered more unique, such as model airplane flying, horseback riding, or the family shooting range.

This popular park often reaches capacity on summer weekends. Off-peak periods such as weekdays, before or after work, early spring, and late fall are less crowded, offering a more peaceful experience. With trails along grasslands, cottonwood trees, and marshes, and mule deer and great horned owls inhabiting the park year-round, winter months are a tranquil treat for hikers, wildlife watchers, and nature lovers. Bike lanes provide a popular year-round workout.

As the water table rose along Cherry Creek and tributary drainages, around the reservoir, and below the dam, it established sizeable and diverse wetlands, cottonwood riparian habi-

Cherry Creek State Park

tats, and aquatic plant communities. This ecosystem attracts raptor species such as golden eagle, red-tailed hawk, northern harrier, and ferruginous hawk, as well as waterfowl and shorebirds. In winter, you might see majestic bald eagles perched on the cottonwoods or soaring over the water. More than 40 mammal species exist throughout the park, including eastern cottontail rabbit, coyote, beaver, muskrat, raccoon, weasel, and ground squirrel. Though dependent on season, dawn and dusk are usually the best times for viewing wildlife. Visitors often see whitetailed deer and scampering black-tailed prairie dogs, but you also might catch a glimpse of the plains garter snake, western hognose snake, or even a bull snake or rattlesnake, which are often difficult to tell apart. *www.parks.state.co.us*

Cherry Creek Regional Trail parallels Cherry Creek, and runs four miles through Cherry Creek State Park. Eventually, the trail will connect with Castlewood Canyon State Park 24 miles to the south. Along the way, it also will connect various local park and open space properties, and the communities of

Parker, Centennial, and Franktown. Part of the Colorado Front Range Trail, CCRT is a multi-use trail, although no gas-powered motors are allowed. Dogs are welcome, but must remain on leash. Trailheads are located off Parker Road to the west at Cherry Creek State Park, Cottonwood Park, Bar Triple C Park in Parker, Salisbury Park, West Bank Park south of Parker, the North Pinery Trailhead, Hidden Mesa Open Space, and Castlewood Canyon State Park. There's a good map at *www.douglas.co.us/parksandtrails*

Cherry Creek Spillway Trail provides offstreet connections to Cherry Creek State Park and the Cherry Creek Regional Trail. The

east access for the Spillway Trail is in Aurora at Chambers Road and Yale Avenue, just across from Olympic Park. Once inside the state park, get on the Cherry Creek Trail and head west all the way to the South Platte in Denver, 13 miles away. There's no fee if you walk or ride your bike into the park. Access the Spillway Trail from the west at the Parker Road underpass for Hampden Avenue. There's a great map at *www.auroragov.org*.

Cherry Creek Valley Ecological Park is a 75-acre natural ecological reserve located south of Cherry Creek State Park in the wilderness area between Parker and Jordan roads along the Cherry Creek Regional Trail. Crusher fine trails wind to overlooks of the small pond and meandering Cherry Creek. You can stroll along the wood boardwalk that crosses the wetlands and view the pond from a small overlook. Interpretive signage within the park gives the visitor a glimpse of local natural and cultural history. Other amenities include: trailhead parking area, school bus turn-around/student drop-off, covered picnic gazebo, outdoor classroom, and restrooms. In an effort to protect water quality and wildlife, dogs must be on a leash and are not permitted in some areas. Go east on Broncos Parkway from Jordan Road and take the first left on East Jamison Drive. Turn right on East Jasper Court, which dead ends at the park. *www.co.arapahoe.co.us*

17 Mile House Farm Park is an Arapahoe County designated Heritage Area that includes an 1860s-era mile house, silo, and barn along the historic Cherokee Trail stagecoach route to Denver. This park is scheduled to open to the public in 2013. Today, the 17 Mile House

Cherry Creek Valley Ecological Park

and barn look much like they did 120 years ago, and the County is working to restore the historic structures. The 17 Mile House has a long and significant history. When the 1859-1860 Gold Rush resulted in the large-scale settlement of Colorado, six way stations emerged along Cherry Creek to accommodate travelers. These mile houses were located every two to three miles along the Cherokee/Smoky Hill Trails, all leading to and named based on the distance to the intersection of Colfax Avenue and Broadway in Denver. Upon arrival, travelers could get meals, spend the night, rest their animals, and have minor repairs made to their coaches or wagons. Out of the original six mile houses, only 17 Mile House and 4 Mile House, located at 715 South Forest Street, exist in their entirety today.

The 17 Mile House property is situated between Douglas County's 75-acre Norton Farm Open Space, the town of Parker, and the recently acquired 107-acre Parker Jordan Centennial Open Space. These three adjoining open space properties serve as a regional wildlife corridor and provide key habitat for deer, coyote, and raptors. *www.co.arapahoe.co.us*

Greenwood Village

A hidden treasure tucked away in the heart of rural Greenwood Village, the **Marjorie Perry Nature Preserve** is surrounded by 1.5 miles of one of Colorado's premier trail networks, the Highline Canal. Nestled in a sharp bend of the trail near the intersection of East Belleview Avenue and South Colorado Boulevard, the Marjorie Perry Nature Preserve consists of 55 acres of extraordinary natural beauty in the heart of Denver's southern metro area. I've been photographing it for 30 years! Whether passing through stands of cottonwood trees; traveling past ponds, wetlands, and grasslands; catching a glimpse of the birds and wildlife that find safe haven here; or simply enjoying wonderful views of the Front Range; walkers, joggers, bikers, and horseback riders consider this preserve to be a treasured resource. It's also a perfect location for artists and photography buffs to capture nature's beauty. Access to this stretch of the Highline Canal Trail and the preserve is somewhat limited since it's located in the middle of a residential development called The Preserve. A detailed map is available at *www.greenwoodvillage.com*.

Littleton

As the cities around it have grown, the South Platte River has become a focal point for local conservation. The **South Platte Greenway Legacy Project,** extending from Englewood to the Arapahoe County line south of Littleton, protects many of the river's original natural features, including riparian habitat, wetlands, trees, vegetation, ponds, and wildlife. This stretch of the river is one of my favorite urban places to photograph, if not just to get away from the city hustle and bustle. The birdlife is amazing along the river and the deciduous tree scenery is incredibly photogenic, especially in May and October. The South Suburban Parks and Recreation District manages much of this domain.

The **Mary Carter Greenway** features an eight-mile, multi-use trail with whitewater boating access along the South Platte River. The greenway forms an integral part of the central spine of the Denver metro area greenway sys-

tem and is enjoyed by more than 700,000 users each year. See maps at *www.ssprd.org*.

One of the first natural flood plain parks in the nation, **South Platte Park** is the result of four decades of partnership between the City of Littleton, South Suburban Park and Recreation District, U.S. Army Corps of Engineers, the Colorado Water Conservation Board, Littleton citizens, and numerous private property owners. Extensively gravel-mined for

South Platte Park

more than 30 years and now reclaimed, the 100-year flood plain park is home to more than 246 species of birds and 23 species of fish. Besides this rich diversity of resident and migratory wildlife, the park also hosts more than 350,000 visitors a year. The **Carson Nature Center** serves as the park's interpretive facility. *www.ssprd.org/nature*

A crucial keystone property between several adjoining open space properties already owned by the City of Littleton, **Lee Gulch** provides important connections to the Lee Gulch Trail and the Mary Carter Greenway. The Lee Gulch Trail begins at the Mary

Carter Greenway Trail at the confluence of the South Platte River and Lee Gulch, which is south of Highway 85 and West Ridge Road in Littleton, and ends at the C-470 East Trail in Littleton. *www.ssprd.org*

The 28-acre **Wynetka Ponds Park** is located at South Lowell Boulevard and West Bowles Avenue. It features athletic fields, trails, natural open space and the "Bark Park," which may not be the fanciest dog park in the Denver area, but the dogs don't seem to mind. Even if you don't have a pooch, there's plenty of entertainment to be had in observing the doggy antics. *www.ssprd.org*

Wynetka Ponds Park

Douglas County
Parker

The Town of Parker made its first open space acquisition in 1999 with the purchase of the **Norton Farm Open Space.** This 72-acre property, located along Cherry Creek on the west side of Parker Road at the Arapahoe County line, serves as a buffer from development to the north. For the past few decades, the Norton property has served as a horse boarding, breeding, and training facility. The Norton trailhead site is the northern gateway into the Parker community and Douglas County. The Cherry Creek Trail crosses the west side of the property and is bordered on both sides by mature cottonwood trees. *www.douglas.co.us/openspace*

O'Brien Park features a lighted softball field, basketball court, playground, and an outdoor pool with slides and other water features. The park's gazebo serves as the backdrop for many Parker events, including outdoor concerts and the Mayor's Tree Lighting. O'Brien Park is located on the northeast corner of Parker Road and Main Street. Access the parking lot from Victorian Drive. *www.parkeronline.org*

Salisbury Equestrian Park is a 160-acre facility that serves Parker's equestrian community, as well as a variety of youth and adult sports leagues. Thirty acres of the park are undeveloped open space. Youth baseball fields sponsored by the Colorado Rockies are located on the north side of the park. Salisbury's playground encourages creative play, with a non-traditional modern design that appeals to big and little kids alike. Salisbury Park's equestrian facility features a lighted arena with bleacher seating for approximately 80 people, warm-up and dressage arenas, and a two-story equestrian building that includes an office/ticket area, restrooms, and a judges' observation room. From the intersection of Parker Road and Main Street, go west on Main Street 1.2 miles to Motsenbocker Road. Turn south on Motsenbocker and go 2.1 miles. Salisbury Park is on the east side of Motsenbocker, north of the town's public works facility. You can reach Salisbury Equestrian Park from the east by the Cherry Creek Trail near the McCabe Meadows trailhead. *www.parkeronline.org*

Highlands Ranch

The **East-West Regional Trail** will eventually connect Chatfield State Park with the town of Parker. The proposed finished length of this natural surface trail will be approximately 26 miles. Twelve of the 17 miles of existing trail winds through the grasslands and oak bluffs of the 8,200-acre Highlands Ranch Backcountry Wilderness Area, a conserved open space. The views to the Front Range are simply sublime. The ubiquitous oak brush is magnificent green in May and takes on an otherworldly orange and red in October. Though this wilderness area is available only to residents of the community, the East-West Regional Trail is open to the public. Hiking, horseback riding, mountain biking, and dogs on leashes are allowed. The completed portion of the trail extends from Redstone Park in Highlands Ranch east to Bluffs Regional Park in Lone Tree. From C-470, exit south on University Boulevard. Turn right on Wildcat Reserve Parkway, then left on McArthur Ranch Road. Take the next right at Griggs Road, which becomes Daniels Park Road heading south. Drive south two miles to the trailhead on the left. Or, from Highway 85/Santa Fe Drive, take Daniels Park Road

East-West Regional Trail

north five miles to Griggs Road. The trailhead will be on the right. Several other trailheads exist. There's a restroom and a picnic shelter at the Griggs Road Trailhead. See the maps at *www.douglas.co.us/parksandtrails.*

Littleton:
Roxborough Complex

Not far to the south of Jefferson County's Chatfield State Park (see page 74) is an area I include in my personal top 10 places on Earth to visit and photograph. This is not hyperbole! When I lived full time in Denver and couldn't get up to the hills, **Roxborough State Park** was my favorite place to retreat. Roxborough is unlike any other place I've seen. Red sandstone fins rise up to silhouette against the cobalt blue sky; deciduous trees turn red, orange, and yellow in the fall; and wildflowers decorate the short grass prairie—these are just a few of the features that make this area unique. Add the red light of a summer sunrise and this park is aflame. Like Chatfield, a large network of buffering lands and trails surround the park.

Roxborough State Park is a designated Colorado Natural Area, National Cultural District, and National Natural Landmark.

Located along the foothills of the Rocky Mountains in the ecotone between plains grassland and Front Range forest communities, the park encompasses 3,329 acres with elevations ranging from 5,900 to 7,280 feet above sea level. Willow Creek, Little Willow Creek, and Mill Gulch are the park's primary drainages. While dramatic hogbacks, spires, and monoliths encompass the landscape, the most striking feature for Roxborough visitors is the dramatic Fountain Formation, a spectacular tilted sandstone that began more than 300 million years ago with the gradual uplift and erosion of the Ancestral Rocky Mountains. Today, these red sandstones stand majestically at a 60-degree angle.

The park contains high-quality and relatively undisturbed examples of several natural communities, including ponderosa pine, woodlands, Douglas-fir forests, Gambel oak thickets, and tall- and mixed-grass prairie. Cottonwoods and a few aspens can also be found here. Visitors to Roxborough often see mule deer, black-tailed prairie dog, coyote, cottontail rabbit, red fox, and rock squirrel. Occasional observations of elk and black bear, and rare sightings of mountain lions and bobcats also occur. Roxborough's bird

Roxborough State Park

list—a compilation of more than 20 years of observation—contains 145 species, 42 of which nest in the park, including raptors, songbirds, waterfowl, and grassland species such as vesper sparrow and western meadowlark. Among other birds, you might also see canyon wren, western tanager, and broadtailed hummingbirds, as well as sensitive species such as ferruginous hawks and burrowing owls. Look closely for the golden eagle nest located on the Fountain Formation just outside of the park boundary.

Camping, mountain bikes, pets, and horses are not allowed in the park. Take Wadsworth south past Chatfield State Park and turn left on Waterton Road (just before the entrance to Lockheed Martin). Continue on Waterton Road, crossing the South Platte River, until it ends at North Rampart Range Road. Turn south on North Rampart Range Road and continue past Roxborough Village and the Foothills Water Treatment Plant. At the intersection of North Rampart Range Road and Roxborough Park Road, just before the entrance to Arrowhead Golf Club, turn left onto Roxborough Park Road. Take the next right (about 50 yards away) to enter the park. *www.parks.state.co.us*

Sharptail Ridge Open Space and State Wildlife Area protects the scenic viewshed and wildlife habitat east of Roxborough State Park. The 4.6 Sharptail Trail crosses rolling grasslands that are home to a variety of wildlife, including elk herds. Seasonal closures of this natural surface trail occur in the fall to allow for hunting, as regulated by the Colorado Division of Parks and Wildlife. Look for great views back to the red rocks and the Rampart Range. Hiking and horseback riding are allowed on the trail, but bicycling and dogs are not. At the trailhead, you'll find a log cabin-style group picnic shelter, a port-a-potty, parking for cars and horse trailers, interpretive signage, hitching rails, benches, and a water spigot. Follow the directions to Roxborough State Park, but after turning left onto Roxborough Road, instead of taking the next right to enter the park, continue east two-thirds of a mile. The trailhead will be on your right. Good maps are available at *www.douglas.co.us/openspace*.

The 695-acre **Nelson Ranch Open Space** and the 308-acre Pike Hill Open Space are located south of Roxborough State Park, behind the hogback. Helping to buffer the park's attributes, these open spaces also create connectivity to this scenic landscape. The open space designation protects a variety of wildlife habitats that thrive among the Gambel oaks, ponderosa pines, Douglas-firs, hawthorn and chokecherry bushes, and narrow-leaved cottonwoods. This area offers excellent opportunities for dispersed, passive public recreation, such as hiking, horseback riding, and mountain biking (for this use, access only from Pike National Forest). Pike Hill Open Space rises from the western side of Nelson Ranch and serves as a connection between County open space and Pike National Forest. Ringtail and Swallowtail Trails pervade these open spaces and connect with Sharptail Trail to the north. You can start at Sharptail and work your way south, or better yet, start at the Indian Creek Trailhead in Pike National Forest. From Highway 85/Santa Fe Drive at Sedalia, take Highway 67 west 11 miles to the campground and trailhead. Ringtail Trail begins 1.6 miles north of the trailhead. Remember, horses and hikers only if accessing from Sharptail Trail; mountain bikes and leashed dogs if accessing from Indian Creek Trail. *www.douglas.co.us/openspace*.

After your hike, take the kids to **Roxborough Village Skate Park,** voted *Westword* magazine's

Nelson Ranch Open Space

Best Skate Park in 2010. Head south on Santa Fe Drive to Titan Road, then west on Titan Road, which becomes Rampart Range Road. The skate park will be on the west side of the road just past the gas station. Pull into the parking lot right after the row of houses. *www.roxboroughmetrodistrict.org*

Castle Pines

Elk Ridge Park offers something for every person and every generation. Considered a multi-generational and multi-accessible park, it's designed to accommodate family play, all-generation play, and multi-ability play for children. From I-25, take the Castle Pines Parkway Exit 188. Go one-half mile and make a left on Lagae Road. Take the first right onto Mira Vista Lane to the park. *www.cpnmd.org*

Castle Rock

If you're traveling along I-25 with the kids, **Paintbrush Park** is a great place to take a break. Not only is the playground fantastic, but the park also features a baseball field, bike path, climbing wall, picnic tables, and sand volleyball court. Located at 3492 Meadows Boulevard, take the Founders Parkway/Meadows Parkway Exit 184 off I-25, and go west one mile. Meadows Parkway becomes Meadows Boulevard. Continue straight 1.5 miles to the park on your right.

Quarry Mesa Open Space is a 133-acre protected area on the west side of Rhyolite Regional Park. This was the site of the town's first Rhyolite stone quarry, which opened in 1872. From the top of the grassland mesa, visitors can enjoy spectacular views of Douglas County and the Front Range, from Pikes Peak to Longs Peak. The **Madge Trail** system features more than three miles of natural surface looped trails for hikers, runners, and mountain bikers. Parking is available at Rhyolite Regional Park. From I-25, take the Wolfensberger/Wilcox Exit 182 east onto Wilcox Street and travel 1.5 miles. Where Wilcox becomes Frontage Road, go 1.6 miles, then turn left onto Crystal Valley Parkway. The park is another 2.1 miles on the left. Follow the paved trail to the natural surface trail.

East Plum Creek Trail is a 5.3-mile paved trail that takes users through the wetland and riparian habitat of lower Sellars Gulch and East Plum Creek. Part of the Colorado Front Range Trail, this trail functions as both a recreational and commuter trail, providing access between The Meadows and downtown Castle Rock, as well as Founders Village and

Paintbrush Park

Quarry Mesa Open Space

Castlewood Ranch. The Meadows portion offers a prime birdwatching location, and an interpretive station and educational materials have been installed to help trail users with identification. Parking is available on Meadows Parkway, with additional parking at Festival Park and along South Perry Street. From I-25, take the Founders Parkway/Meadows Parkway Exit 184 west onto Meadows Parkway. The trailhead parking lot is one-half mile on your left.

East Plum Creek Trail

Gateway Mesa Open Space lies on a bluff, with steep, rock-capped cliffs on the eastern portion overlooking Franktown and the Cherry Creek valley to the east. The property has expansive views of the Rocky Mountains, extending from Pikes Peak to the south, to Longs Peak to the northwest. Beware of steep cliffs and rattlesnakes while hiking the natural surface, 1.8-mile **Chuck's Loop Trail,** which connects to the Mitchell Creek Trail System. Mountain bikes and horses are not permitted on this trail. From I-25, take the Founders Parkway/Meadows Parkway Exit 184 east onto Founders Parkway for 4.4 miles. Turn left onto Highway 86 and then right at two miles into the dirt driveway to the trailhead parking lot. Visit *www.crgov.com* for information and maps for each of these Castle Rock properties.

Greenland Complex

The **Greenland Ranch Open Space** system, aka the **I-25 Conservation Corridor,** is a huge collection of properties along I-25. Providing a natural area surrounding the interstate, the open space properties extend between Castle Rock and Monument Hill from north to south, and between Perry Park Road and Highway 83 from west to east. Douglas County has already preserved about 34,000 acres in this area, which means there will always be a portion of the Front Range prairie grasslands and buttes between Colorado Springs and Denver, and that Colorado's two largest cities will never become one!

Much of the land has been preserved under conservation easements that allow the area east of I-25, the Greenland Ranch, to remain a working ranch. The 4,000+-acre section west of I-25, Greenland Open Space and Spruce Mountain, are open to the public and can be enjoyed via wonderful trails. Part of the Colorado Front Range Trail, **Greenland Open Space Trail** joins the Old Territorial Road, which connects the old Greenland town site to Palmer Lake. The trail passes through native grasslands, by ponds, through rolling Gambel oak hills, skirts ponderosa pine forests, and offers great views of the Greenland buttes and Pikes Peak. This is one of my favorite places on the plains to photograph at sunrise! Because the rising sun illuminates everything in its path with warm yellow light, make certain to arrive before sunrise in order to catch the first and best 10 minutes of light. To reach the trailhead, take I-25 to Greenland Exit 167 south of Larkspur. Go west on Noe Road about one-quarter mile and follow the road south to the huge gate. A large parking complex has been built and the picnic shelter

is set-up to handle horses. The total trail distance from the parking lot and around the loop is 8.2 miles. A secondary trailhead can be reached by taking the County Line Road/Palmer Lake Exit 163 from I-25 and heading two miles west on County Line Road. More information and a map are available at *www.douglas.co.us/openspace.*

Dawson Butte Ranch Open Space

The five-mile loop trail at **Dawson Butte Ranch Open Space** travels over gently rolling terrain through mostly forested areas of ponderosa pine and Gambel oak. Along the way, you'll pass through some open meadows and catch great views of Front Range mountains. Don't expect to reach the top of the butte because there is no access. Hiking, mountain biking, snowshoeing, and leashed pets are allowed, as well as horseback riding with optional bridal paths including over 60 horse jumps. From I-25, take the Plum Creek Parkway exit west and head south five miles on the frontage road. Turn west at Tomah Road and proceed 1.5 miles to the Dawson Butte Ranch entrance on the right. *www.douglas.co.us/openspace*

Spruce Mountain Trail ascends Spruce Mountain through a ponderosa pine and Douglas-fir forest. The first lookout offers breathtaking views of Greenland Open Space, surrounding buttes, Pikes Peak, the Palmer Divide, Carpenter Creek, and thousands of acres of protected open space. The trail offers plenty of opportunities to gaze in all directions from rocky lookouts. Bring both the wide angle

Greenland Ranch

Spruce Mountain Trail overlook

and telephoto lenses for this hike! The 5.5 mile round trip is a shady hike on a natural surface that will take you to a wide and gentle trail that circles the top of the mountain. Ice and snow can build up on the shaded trails. You will encounter switchbacks on the ascent and back down again. Small children have been known to hike it well, but keep an eye on them at the rocky lookouts! For variety, descend on the service road and hike back along the Eagle Pass trail, or try out the 2-mile loop that extends toward County Road 105 to the west.

The parking lot accommodates cars and light trucks only. Although there's no room for horse trailers, they can be parked at the large Spruce Meadows Trailhead along Noe Road to the northeast, adding a couple of miles in each direction to your ride. Water is available at stock ponds along the Spruce Meadows Trail and at the nearby Greenland Open Space Trailhead. From I-25, take the Greenland Exit 167 west and travel one-quarter mile, then one-half mile south. Bypass the Greenland Trailhead and continue right on the main gravel road (Noe Road) over two sets of railroad tracks. Continue another mile to Spruce Mountain Road and turn left. Head south for about one mile to the parking area on your right. See maps at *www.douglas.co.us/openspace*.

Spruce Meadows Trail cuts through undulating fields of grasses and wildflowers as it winds through the grassy meadows between Greenland Open Space and Spruce Mountain. The trail crosses both Spruce Mountain Road and Noe Road before looping back to the parking area. This is an easy 8.5-mile, natural surface trail with minimal elevation gain. A large gravel parking lot will accommodate scores of horse trailers. From I-25, take the Greenland Exit 167 west and travel one-quarter mile, then one-half mile south. Bypass the Greenland Trailhead and continue right on the main gravel road (Noe Road) over two sets of railroad tracks. The parking area is just up a short hill on your left, on the south side of the road. Good maps are available at *www.douglas.co.us/openspace*. All three of these trails allow foot, mountain bike, and horse traffic, and pets on leashes.

Greenland Ranch encapsulates one of the largest undeveloped tracts of land between Denver and Colorado Springs, and more importantly, is virtually unchanged since its beginnings before the turn of the century. In 2000, the 22,000-acre property was purchased by the Conservation Fund in a partnership with Great Outdoors Colorado, Douglas County, the Colorado Division of Parks and Wildlife, and a local rancher. The land was protected via conservation easements and a very limited development plan, which preserves its original integrity for perpetuity. Even though the ranch isn't accessible to the public, views of the ranch from **Upper Lake Gulch Road** with Pikes Peak in the background are just like those seen from the middle of the ranch. From I-25, take the first exit north of Greenland Exit 172, and head east. Be sure to look behind you to the southwest for the best vantages and photographs right off the road. The oaks are a lime-green color in May, and turn brilliant shades of orange and red in October.

You can continue east on Upper Lake Gulch Road all the way to Castlewood Canyon Road, and to the west or backside of **Castlewood Canyon State Park.** A designated Colorado Natural Area, this state park encompasses 2,136 acres within the northernmost extension of the Black Forest. The Black Forest, also known as the Palmer Divide, refers to an elevated peninsula that juts eastward from the Front Range and divides the drainages of the Platte and Arkansas rivers. The Black Forest is a unique ecological region because it borders Front Range foothills and plains grasslands ecosystems. Elevations in Castlewood range between 6,200 to 6,600 feet, with Cherry Creek flowing through its center.

When I lived full time in Denver, Castlewood Canyon—much like Roxborough—was one of my day-trip destinations if I couldn't get up to the hills. There's so much to see and photograph! Vantages with snow-capped Pikes Peak in the background, yellow sandstone canyon walls (some good for rock climbing), and diverse forests of Douglas-fir, ponderosa pine, colorful scrub oak, and even a few hidden caches of aspen all make for spectacular photos. Because the park sits between prairie and montane communities, a mixture of wildlife species representative of both ecotypes can be found at Castlewood, including mule deer, coyote, cottontail rabbit, porcupine, ground squirrel, and red fox. Black bear, mountain lion, and elk are not residents, but occasionally migrate through the area. By combining easy to moderate hikes, avid hikers or leisurely walkers will appreciate more than 13 miles of trails, which travel both above the canyon and in the bottom along the cooling waters of Cherry Creek. I love the plunge pools as the water descends the canyon. To reach the main entrance of the park, take I-25 to Castle Rock and exit onto Founders Parkway eastbound. Take Founders Parkway to Highway 86 and go east four miles to Franktown. Turn south on Highway 83/South Parker Road and travel five miles to the main park entrance. Or, you can enter the park from its west side, as I described above. *www.parks.state.co.us*

Castlewood Canyon State Park

Jefferson County

Thanks to residents, the Jefferson County Open Space program is one of the premier open space programs in the country. In 1972, the citizens of Jefferson County believed so strongly in the need to preserve open space that they voted to tax themselves one-half of one percent on sales to fund planning, acquiring, maintaining, and preserving open space properties. In 1980, an election expanded the use of open space funds to allow for the construction, maintenance, and management of park and recreation facilities. This enabled the program to provide campgrounds at White Ranch and Reynolds Parks, multiple sports facilities at Clement Park, and contributed to the development of several publicly-owned athletic fields, playgrounds, swimming pools, golf courses, picnic shelters, restrooms, recreation centers, regional parks and trails. In 1998, with more than 70 percent support, Jeffco voters authorized $160 million in general obligation bonds to fund acquisition of priority properties. Since 1972, the cities and unincorporated areas of the county have spent more than $285 million to acquire roughly 51,000 acres of land, water, and facilities. *www.jeffco.us*

Golden

A work-in-progress, the **Clear Creek Corridor Project** is designed to help protect and provide public access to Clear Creek Canyon in Clear Creek and Jefferson counties. Jeffco's **Clear Creek Canyon Park** is abundant in both recreation and historical resources. The Jefferson County segment of the canyon plays a critical role in the completion of a trail system extending from the Continental Divide to the prairie. Recreational opportunities, such as hiking, climbing, rafting, kayaking, and cave exploration, will be monitored to ensure sustainability of natural resources. Maintaining the canyon's historical integrity through interpretation, education, and

Clear Creek Canyon Park

Centennial Cone Park

preservation of historical uses, including gold panning and streamside picnicking, is also a high priority.

Grant Terry Park is the first segment of this long-term trail project through Clear Creek Canyon Park. Located just west of Golden and Highway 6, Grant Terry Park was previously inaccessible to the public until a bridge was constructed across Clear Creek. Over time, Jeffco plans to build a trail through the

canyon to Clear Creek County and the Continental Divide Trail. The Clear Creek Canyon Trail project stretches more than 12 miles through a narrow creek corridor over difficult terrain, and will require time and investment of funds to complete. *www.jeffco.us*

Centennial Cone Park provides valuable habitat for elk, mountain lion, and other species. Located north of Clear Creek Canyon, near the Clear Creek County line, the park's natural

surface trail system is designed to offer visitors a backcountry-type experience. Because trail users have endorsed options to reduce conflict, Centennial Cone Park has implemented an alternating-use schedule that separates hikers and bikers on the weekends. Limited elk and deer hunting in December and January helps ensure herd populations that are in harmony with available habitat. Seasonal closures may occur during the elk calving period so that a certain portion of the park has minimal disturbance by humans. *www.jeffco.us*

North Table Mountain Park is located just northeast of the city of Golden. With several miles of spectacular, existing trails and more under construction, the 1,969-acre park is a work-in-progress. The flat-topped North Table Mountain rises almost 1,000 feet above the surrounding plains with very steep side slopes. The mountain is the result of three lava flows that originated from the Ralston Dike located about two miles northwest of the mountain. After centuries of weathering, North Table Mountain has been transformed into an area that contains several different types of habitat, including grasslands, shrub communities, lichen rock gardens, riparian, shore, and cliff. Although human activity has occurred over the years, the park's habitat is still considered high-quality, and in 1993 the Colorado Natural Heritage Program classified North Table Mountain as one of only 27 conservation sites in the county.

Home to prairie dogs and more than 80 mule deer, the mountain also provides habitat for golden eagles and red-tailed hawks. Shore birds and ducks can be seen around the three ponds dotting the top of the mountain. These spring-fed ponds are the headwaters of two major drainages on the mountain, which form narrow bands of riparian vegetation that almost completely bisect the property. A seasonal closure in effect from March 15 to July 31 each year helps protect several species of

cliff-nesting raptors that rely upon the mesa cliffs for habitat to raise their young. A parking area at the trailhead is located north of Golden on Highway 93, just north of Pine Ridge Road. *www.jeffco.us*

South Table Mountain Park is also a work-in-progress. The dominant features of this park are the unusual rock outcroppings that characterize the mesas of the Golden area. Initially, only a small portion of the mesa on the east side was owned and managed by Jeffco. Now, less than 400 acres remain in private ownership. Conservation easements on state, federal, and private lands provide trail connections, and park visitors are asked to respect private property boundaries. The park features several miles of trail, but neighborhood access at the west terminus of Foothills Circle is limited. Visit *www.jeffco.us* for a map and updated information.

The seven-acre **Maple Grove Park** features a playground, one baseball/softball diamond, two regulation-size youth football fields, one basketball court, a volleyball court, a horseshoe pit, and the **Arbor House** community building. For picnicking, choose from three

Crestview Park features two unique play areas for children of different ages, as well as a picnic pavilion, grassy play areas, and benches. It's located at 5401 Juniper Court, north of 52nd Avenue and east of McIntyre Street. *www.prospectdistrict.org*

More than 12,000 acres of dense forest, rocky peaks, and aspen-rimmed meadows laced with miles of trails await the hiker, horseback rider, mountain biker, and winter sports enthusiast at **Golden Gate State Park.** Only 30 miles from Denver, Golden Gate Canyon offers amenities such as electrical hook-ups and tent sites in two different campgrounds, stocked fishing ponds, picnic sites, and the Panorama Point Scenic Overlook where visitors can view 100 miles of the Continental Divide. Wintertime showcases cross-country skiing, snowshoeing, sledding, ice fishing, and ice skating opportunities.

The park is home to an abundance of wildlife, including mule deer, elk, black bear, mountain lion, bobcat, coyote, raccoon, striped skunk, snowshoe hare, cottontail rabbit, porcupine, muskrat, Abert's and pine squirrel, ground squirrel, and red fox. Creeks throughout the park support cold-water fishing species such as brook and rainbow trout, with the latter also stocked in put-and-take ponds. Also thriving in the park are many species of migratory and resident birds, including songbirds, waterfowl, and raptors— the most common of which are the turkey vulture, red-tailed hawk, and American kestrel. The golden eagle and ferruginous

shelters scattered throughout the property. Located at 14600 West 32nd Avenue, the park is about one mile west of I-70 and Youngfield on 32nd Avenue. *www.prospectdistrict.org*

Golden Gate State Park

hawk are less commonly seen. Keen bird-watchers also commonly observe the mountain bluebird, mountain chickadee, common flicker, Gray and Steller's jays, Clark's nutcracker, black-billed magpie, raven, and common nighthawk.

In addition to traditional campground camping at Golden Gate, several other overnight options exist. Since 2008, park guests seeking a bit more comfort have rented the four-bedroom guesthouse—a first in a Colorado State Park. Also available for rental are five cabins and two yurts within Reverends' Ridge Campground. Those wanting a more primitive and somewhat unique camping experience might consider one of the park's four backcountry shelters. Built in the Appalachian trail-hut tradition, these three-sided structures with roofs and wood floors can sleep up to six people. Another backcountry option requires backpacking to one of the 20 tent sites, many located in large, scenic meadows surrounded by 10,000-foot peaks.

Over 35 miles of hiking trails in Golden Gate Canyon offer fun and challenges for a variety of skill levels. Each of the park's 12 trails are named after an animal and marked with the animal's footprint (such as Snowshoe Hare Trail and Coyote Trail). Mountain bikes and horses are permitted in the park on multiple-use trails. Ample parking space for horse trailers is provided at the Nott Creek trailhead, located near the Red Barn Group Picnic Area, and at Kriley Overlook above Kriley Pond. Other trailhead parking areas are easily accessible from the main park roads. Take Highway 93 north from Golden one mile to Golden Gate Canyon Road. Turn left and continue for 13 miles to the park. *www.parks.state.co.us*

The **Lookout Mountain Nature Center** promotes awareness, understanding, and conservation of Jefferson County's open spaces through year-round educational programs and exhibits. The center offers something for everyone, including individuals, groups, youth and families. Join a naturalist-led activity to learn more about your favorite nature subject or other guided programs to discover the many natural treasures throughout Jeffco's open space parks. Explore interactive nature exhibits; search the facility for recycled, reused, and earth-friendly building materials; or browse the nature books, gifts, and toys. Stroll the self-guided nature trail and search for wildlife or the clues they leave behind, or scout for wildlife while hiking the

one-and-a-half miles of gently rolling trails. Picnic under towering ponderosa pine trees, and photograph scenic views of Pike's Peak. The Lookout Mountain Trail links to Apex and Windy Saddle Parks, Beaver Brook Trail, and Buffalo Bill's Museum and Grave. Westbound off I-70, take Exit 256 and turn right. Eastbound, use Exit 254 and turn left. Then follow the brown highway signs. *www.jeffco.us*

Evergreen

North Evergreen Activity Trail makes a safe passageway for local school kids walking and biking to and from school to their homes and after-school activities. It also links area homes to recreation and commercial destinations in Bergen Park. The NEAT Trail is a 1.8-mile paved path along Bergen Parkway, running from Evergreen Middle School on Hiwan Drive, through the Bergen Park commercial

corridor, to Bergen Valley Elementary on Sugarbush Drive. The trail has three sections: the Meadow Trail (from the middle school to Broadmoor Drive); the Village Trail (Broadmoor to Bergen Village on Sugarbush); and the Valley Trail (Sugarbush to the elementary school). *www.neatevergreen.org*

Westminster

You can see an amazing variety of wild animals within the 2,000 acres of open space at **Standley Lake Regional Park.** The lake is an artificial reservoir created in the middle of the shortgrass prairie, and the result is a wonderful contrast between prairie, lake, and wetland ecosystems. At the lake, bird watchers can observe many water birds such as white pelicans, western grebes, cormorants, gulls, Canadian geese, and mallard ducks. In 2001—the first time in recent years—great blue herons were found nesting by the lake. Another lake dweller and one of the park's most famous residents, the beaver uses both the lake and the prairie around it. For several years, Standley Lake has been home to a pair of nesting bald eagles. During the summer, the bald eagles fish in the lake; in winter, when the lake freezes over, the eagles steal prairie dogs caught by other birds of prey. Raptors seen at the park include Swainson's Hawks, prairie falcons, and red-tailed hawks, as well as nesting great horned owls, which are night birds of prey. Prairie dogs are a common sight in the open spaces around the lake. In fact, prairie dog towns provide food and shelter for more than 100 species of animals. Bald eagles, coyotes, red foxes, and bull snakes are a few of the park's animal residents that prey on prairie dogs. Burrowing owls and rabbits live in prairie dog burrows. Other mammals seen in the park include mule deer and rock squirrels.

The park includes two campgrounds, two restroom facilities with outdoor showers and drinking water, and a four-lane boat ramp. The main campground accommodates campers, trailers, and tents, with several sites along the

Standley Lake Regional Park

waterside. All campsites have fire pits and picnic tables. Camping is available May 1 through September 29 on a first-come, first-served basis.

Standley Lake Regional Park boasts more than 14 miles of maintained trails, single-track trails, and roads for hiking, mountain biking, and horseback riding. The few steep hills will reward you with breathtaking over-looks of Standley Lake and the Front Range. The park is also the starting point for some of Westminster's major trail corridors, including the **Big Dry Creek Trail** and the Farmers' High Line Canal Trail. The crown jewel of Westminster's off-road trail system, Big Dry Creek Trail meanders nearly 12 miles from

City and County of Broomfield
Metzger Farm

This 150-acre open space is owned by the Broomfield/Westminster Open Space Foundation and was acquired in 2006. The property is located within Westminster, but is bordered on the west and north by Broomfield. The Metzger Farm is an open space crown jewel with unique natural areas as well as a rich history. Hidden from view are two scenic ponds. The smaller 1.11-acre upper pond is mostly a cattail-filled wetland, while the 4.05-acre lower pond is deep enough to support fish. Both ponds attract a wide variety of water fowl including ducks, Canadian Geese, white egrets, great blue herons, night crested herons and pelicans. East of the lower pond is the Big Dry Creek riparian area. Huge cottonwood trees create a beautiful shady environment that attracts owls and hawks. The farm house and nine farm outbuildings line the north side of the ponds. The farm was mostly used as a cattle grazing operation by the Metzger family, although dairy cows were kept at one point.

The farm will be open to the public in 2012 with a parking lot and over two miles of trails. Visit the City of Westminster's website to check on the status of the farm's opening. *www.cityofwestminster.us*

Standley Lake Regional Park to I-25, crossing under most streets through underpasses. The trail is located on more than 800 acres of Westminster open space and 200 acres of park land along the creek, a land area greater than New York's 843-acre Central Park! The Big Dry Creek Trail was designated a National Recreation Trail in 2003. Go west on 100th Avenue from Wadsworth Parkway to Simms Street, then south to the park. *www.cityofwestminster.us*

The city owns three separate parcels of open space along Walnut Creek, collectively called **Walnut Creek Open Space.** A 14.6-acre open space parcel exists between Highway 36 and

Wadsworth Boulevard along the creek. A .7-mile trail extending from the Big Dry Creek to Wadsworth Boulevard along Walnut Creek provides nice glimpses of the creek and wetland areas. West of Wadsworth Boulevard and east of Wadsworth Parkway, the city owns 36.5 acres of open space and manages an additional 14 acres of land owned by the Nature Conservancy (the Chambers Preserve). This is one of the most beautiful and dramatic open space properties in the city. Although this property provides no formal trails, several informal narrow trails follow Walnut Creek. To access these trails, park near the corner of 104th Avenue and Dover Street. You might want to travel through the 44 acres of open space located north of 108th Avenue and east of Simms Street. The gravel Walnut Creek Trail extends 1.5 miles through this area and offers pastoral views of the creek area. *www.cityofwestminster.us*

Arvada

Gold Strike Park is the site of one of the earliest American gold discoveries in Colorado. The Lewis Ralston Gold Discovery Site was named for the discovery made by Lewis Ralston, a member of a wagon train bound for California in 1850. The Ralston party rested for a day near a then-unnamed stream. Lewis Ralston dipped in his gold pan and came up

with nearly $5 in gold in his first pan. Although the initial gold strike never yielded a large amount of gold, it led to visits by other prospectors, including an 1858 discovery that started Colorado's first gold rush. Head north on Sheridan Boulevard from I-76 to the first traffic light at Ralston Road. Go west to 56th Avenue and left to the park on your left. *www.arvada.org*

Two Ponds National Wildlife Refuge is the smallest urban unit in the National Wildlife Refuge System. The refuge covers 72.2 acres, including 63.2 acres of uplands, nine acres of wetlands, and three small ponds, and contains various types of plant communities. The refuge provides several wildlife-oriented recreational opportunities, including environmental

education programs and guided tours. In addition to more than 113 bird species, deer, turtles, fox, ducks, voles, and other wildlife, visitors can view habitat such as cattails, milkweed, rushes, and willows. Several trails are open to the public seasonally. Take 80th Avenue west past Wadsworth Boulevard. The refuge is located on the south side of 80th Avenue just before Kipling Street. Refuge information is available at the entrance kiosk by the parking area. *www.fws.gov/twoponds*

Long Lake Ranch Park provides active recreational opportunities, including ball fields and trails, while preserving more than half of the site as open space and wildlife habitat. The park encompasses 430 acres of a former working ranch and farm that was first homesteaded in 1862. Its current ecosystem is diverse and includes the remnants of shortgrass prairie. The area is home to a number of different small animals, which raptors and coyotes frequently hunt. Several families of black-tailed prairie dogs also inhabit the park property. Careful consideration was given to wildlife during the park's design, as well as to sensitivity of and connectivity between habitat zones. The **Fairmount Trail,** a Jefferson County Open Space trail, follows a Denver Water Board irrigation canal, starting near the Arvada Reservoir east of Highway 93 on the south edge of 64th Avenue. From there, the trail follows the canal through Long Lake Ranch Regional Park past the historic Churches Ranch, then south along the canal to Easley Road. This trail is entirely soft surface for equestrians, joggers, and mountain bikers. To get to the park from westbound I-70, take Exit 266 north on Ward Road 2.1 miles to 64th Avenue. Go west on 64th Avenue 3.3 miles to the park. *www.arvada.org*

Lake Arbor Community Park's 60 acres includes a 30-acre lake, playground, restroom, fitness trail, fishing docks, picnic tables, pavilion, and one-mile walking track. Just north of West 80th Avenue, head east on Pomona Drive from Wadsworth Boulevard. You'll see the park and lake on the right. *www.arvada.org*

Arvada's only **Skateboard Park** lies in the northeast corner of **Memorial Park.** This facility offers a six-foot half pipe, four-foot half pipe, pyramid, bionic bow, and an ollie box. Take Olde Wadsworth Boulevard north from Ralston Road to Brooks Drive. Go west to the park on your left. *www.arvada.org*

Wheat Ridge

The **Crown Hill Park Open Space** is known for its sweeping mountain views and brilliant sunsets. A wildlife watcher's paradise, this urban park provides excellent opportunities to observe waterfowl and migratory birds,

coyote, and fox. In 1860, Henry and William Lee traveled west from Iowa and homesteaded the land that is now the park. They raised produce to sell to the mining camps along the Front Range. The first apple orchard in Wheat Ridge was established here.

Created in 1979, the 242-acre Crown Hill Park has been kept in a natural state with minimal development. Of the approximately 6.5 miles of available trails here, 3.5 miles are paved and form two major loops. Horseback riding is permitted, but primarily on designated trails in the park's southwest corner. The nature preserve features a .7-mile trail.

In 1991, the now-defunct National Institute for Urban Wildlife dedicated this area as an urban national wildlife refuge. The protected wetlands, centered on nearby Kestrel Pond in the northwest corner of the park, reserves an area that is subject to seasonal closure for the protection of nesting migratory waterfowl. To get there from 6th Avenue, turn north on Kipling to 26th Avenue. The main parking lot is located on 26th Avenue between Garrison and Garland Streets An equestrian lot is located on 26th Avenue. *www.jeffco.us*

Designated in 2007 as a National Recreation Trail, **Clear Creek Trail** has the feel of an eastern forest—unusual for the arid climate of Colorado's Front Range. The 6.5-mile, family-friendly, multi-use trail, located just south of I-70, runs from Harlan Street to Youngfield Street, winding through the scenic Wheat

Clear Creek Trail

Ridge Greenbelt. The Clear Creek Trail provides numerous conservation benefits and recreation opportunities, including biking, walking, kayaking, and bird watching. It passes by a historic fording of Clear Creek known as Boyd's Crossing that was used during the initial gold rush and exploration of Colorado. Clear Creek Trail connects with Golden to the west and the South Platte River Trail to the east (see Adams County). This trail sequencing makes it possible to ride a bike path from Golden to Littleton or Golden to Brighton, accessing the entire metro area trail system. *www.jeffco.us* and *www.ci.wheatridge.co.us*

Prospect Park features a wildlife-viewing boardwalk at Bass Lake, one of four lakes along this stretch of Clear Creek Trail, located on the south side of Clear Creek west of the parking lot. Check it out at 44th Avenue and Robb Street. Take the Ward Road exit from I-70 to 44th Avenue, head east, and the park will be on your right. *www.ci.wheatridge.co.us*

Discovery Park

Bear Creek Lake Park

Using nature as its primary theme, **Discovery Park** has three main areas that offer distinct connections between landscape, nature, and use: The main plaza area and amphitheater connect the sun with a sense of community. The play area's forest theme connects water with play, and the skate park's mountain theme connects wind and play. Discovery Park includes a playground, a climbing wall, and a maze. It's located at 38th Avenue and Kipling Street. *www.ci.wheatridge.co.us*

Lakewood

Bear Creek Lake Park offers an abundance of recreational and educational opportunities. Explore the park by foot, from the deck of a sailboat, on a mountain bike, or on the back of a horse. Swimmers of all ages and abilities enjoy the swim beach at Big Soda Lake. Bring your family and friends and spend a day in the sand, or rent paddleboats, canoes, kayaks, or a sailboard for fun on the water. Rentals are available from Memorial Day to Labor

Day. Novices needing lessons can visit the water ski school at Little Soda Lake. Open year round for fishing, Bear Creek Lake typically is stocked once or twice a month from May through September with rainbow trout, saugeye, small mouth bass, and yellow perch. On occasion, a tiger muskie or walleye also have been caught.

The park has approximately 15 miles of multi-use dirt trails, the majority of which are open to horseback riders. Trails pass through open meadows and along creeks, offer wide-ranging views from Mount Carbon, and connections to the Bear Creek Greenbelt. The park's visitor center conducts educational programming, and its exhibits acquaint visitors with the many wildlife and vegetation species of the Colorado aquatic, riparian, and upland prairie ecosystems. These distinct yet connected ecosystems are presented in three display areas featuring illustrations and wildlife mountings. The park entrance is on the south side of Morrison Road just east of C-470. *www.lakewood.org*

Ray Ross Park has three lighted baseball and softball fields, two lighted football fields, a walking path, a great playground, and a new "spray ground" to cool off the whole family. It's on the east side of Harlan Street between Ohio and West Virginia Avenues. *www.lakewood.org*

Belmar Park is a 127-acre natural parkland administered by the Lakewood Department of Parks and Recreation. Three ecosystems—riparian, swamp, and prairie grassland—as well as the lovely Kountze Lake, provide homes for a variety of waterfowl and birds. Intersecting gravel paths and horse trails cut through the park, and a 3-mile concrete trail follows its perimeter. Other attractions include the Lakewood Heritage Center Museum, opportunities for nature study, historic buildings and artifacts, and a connection to the half-mile **Weir Gulch Trail** through a tunnel under Wadsworth Boulevard. Take Ohio Avenue west from Wadsworth Boulevard to get to the park. *www.lakewood.org*

Morrison

Dinosaur Ridge is one of the world's most famous dinosaur fossil sites. In 1877, Arthur Lakes, a professor at the Colorado School of Mines in Golden, discovered some of the best-known dinosaurs here. These include Apatosaurus, Allosaurus, and Stegosaurus, the Colorado State Fossil. These specimens represent animals that lived 150 million years ago in the late Jurassic Period, also known as "the age of giants." These discoveries sparked an historic dinosaur gold rush that traced the bone-bearing strata, known as the Morrison Formation (named after the Town of Morrison to the south), across a large part of the Rocky Mountain region. This golden age of 19th century dinosaur exploration led to the discovery of many other important sites in the West. Dozens of successful excavations at Dinosaur Ridge, and at the other locations, have stocked many of the world's museums and brought dinosaurs to public attention.

In 1937, during the construction of West Alameda Parkway, dinosaur tracks were discovered on the east side of Dinosaur Ridge in the 100-million-year-old rocks of the Dakota Group, representing the Early Cretaceous Period. These tracks are those of Iguanodon-like, plant-eating dinosaurs and ostrich-sized, meat-eating dinosaurs. Recent research has revealed that these tracks represent only a small part of the extensive track-bearing beds of the Dakota Group that can be traced from Boulder to northern New Mexico. Because these strata represent the shoreline sediments of an ancient seaway that was frequently trampled by dinosaurs, these beds have been called the "Dinosaur Freeway."

In 1989, the nonprofit organization, Friends of Dinosaur Ridge, was formed to address increasing concerns about the preservation of the Dinosaur Ridge site, and to educate the public about the area's resources. In 2004, the Friends opened the Triceratops Trail to the public. Located in reclaimed clay pits, this half-mile trail runs adjacent to what is now the Fossil Trace Golf Club in Golden. Many 68-million-year-old trace fossils can be

found along the trail, including tracks of dinosaurs, mammals, birds, and beetles.

In 1994, the Friends began renovating a house and barn on the historic Rooney Ranch to create the **Dinosaur Ridge Visitor Center.** Today, the former ranch house is a gift shop offering many attractive and educational items related to dinosaurs and geology, and the barn hosts Trek Through Time, an educational exhibit that allows visitors to orient themselves to the natural history of the area before or after their visit to the fossil sites. Each year, Dinosaur Ridge and Triceratops Trail are destinations for close to 100,000 dinosaur enthusiasts, earth scientists, and nature lovers, and have been used by several generations of earth science teachers as outdoor geology labs. The Dinosaur Ridge Visitor Center is located west of the Alameda Parkway exit off C-470. *www.dinoridge.org*

Littleton

Chatfield Reservoir Complex

The region in and around Chatfield Reservoir in Southwest Littleton is one of the most beautiful and photogenic in Colorado. A state park with Denver Botanic Gardens and Denver Audubon Society facilities make this a must-visit region for nature lovers and photographers. **Chatfield State Park,** the centerpiece, is bisected by the Douglas/Jefferson County line. You can escape the gym on Chatfield's many trails by taking a morning jog, exploring natural areas bordering the reservoir, biking through the park, or riding a horse into the sunset. When visitors see Chatfield's beautiful rolling foothills, expansive reservoir, and abundant wildlife, they can't believe the park is located within minutes of the Denver metro area.

Chatfield's large areas of open space and diversity of terrain and vegetation provide habitat for an abundance of wildlife. Deer, elk, bald eagles, and bear have all been spotted in the park, and a variety of small and large mammals, including whitetail and mule deer, coyote, red fox, cottontail rabbits, prairie dogs, and weasels are often sighted.

More than 300 bird species frequent Chatfield, either as permanent residents or migrators, so passionate birdwatchers will want to scope out the Chatfield Bird List (available online). A rookery at the mouth of the South Platte River provides nesting habitat for double-crested cormorants and approximately 80 pairs of great blue herons. The bald eagle, white pelican, and elusive burrowing owl can be observed either as migrants, or as winter or summer residents. Anglers are attracted to Chatfield for the warm- and cold-water fishing opportunities that include walleye, rainbow trout, tiger muskie, smallmouth bass, yellow perch, bluegill, green and blue sunfish, and blue and channel catfish.

Boaters of all types—from water skiers to fishing enthusiasts, to canoeists and sailors—delight in Chatfield Reservoir's waters. Related amenities include boat rentals, a floating restaurant, and a marina. Four campgrounds at Chatfield offer campers their choice of 197 single-family campsites, all furnished with picnic tables, grills, and electrical hookups, and many with full hookups (water, sewer and electric). Campsites are conveniently located within walking distance to the lake, and nearby facilities include flush toilets, hot showers, laundry, centrally-located water, fire rings, and a sanitary waste station. Ten reservable group camping sites also are available. *www.parks.state.co.us*

The **Discovery Pavilion** celebrates the joining of three of the region's major trail systems: the Platte River Trail, the Waterton Canyon/Colorado Trail, and the Highline Canal Trail. With trail information and an interpretive center, the Discovery Pavilion provides visitors with opportunities to learn about trail safety and etiquette, the ecology of the local landscapes, and the role of the South Platte River and water in Colorado's development. The pavilion includes major amenities such as parking for more than 150 vehicles, an attractive sun/storm shelter, grass amphitheater, central plaza, restrooms, and

Chatfield State Park

water fountains. Thousands of indigenous trees and shrubs have been planted as part of the landscaping effort. Adjacent overlooks of Denver Water's historic Kassler Center, Waterton Canyon, and the South Platte River are extraordinary. All improvements have been designed for universal access including people with disabilities.

The **Audubon Center at Chatfield State Park** is an incredible facility providing critical habitat for an abundance of plants and wildlife. Set alongside the South Platte River, the site offers visitors an opportunity to explore forests, shrublands, grasslands, ponds, and wetland ecosystems. On a hike at the Audubon Center, you might encounter prickly pear blooms drying in the sun, red-winged blackbirds singing loudly to defend territories, fresh raccoon tracks in the mud, or grazing mule deer. Designated an Important Bird Area by the National Audubon Society, the park boasts 345 bird species at

various times of year. More than 150 types of butterflies also inhabit the site, along with a wide variety of plants and other wildlife. Originally part of a 5,000-acre working ranch, the site's original stone farmhouse was transformed into a nature center, warmed in the winter by a large fireplace, and offering classroom and exhibit space. The old stone garage, renovated as an outdoor learning lab, features large overhead doors that were added to provide a unique classroom with walls opening into nature. From C-470, exit onto Wadsworth Boulevard. Go south on Wadsworth about 4.4 miles, past the main entrance for Chatfield State Park. Turn east on Waterton Road. Immediately turn left into the first parking lot at the Audubon Center sign. *www.denveraudubon.com*

Incredibly, even more bounty exists for nature lovers near Chatfield State Park. **Denver Botanic Gardens** at Chatfield is a picturesque nature preserve among the grasslands,

Audubon Center at Chatfield State Park

Denver Botanic Gardens at Chatfield

ponds, and cottonwood banks of Deer Creek. Facilities include display gardens, educational exhibits, working beehives, picnic areas, nature trails, a wildlife observation area, historical farm, and 19th-century one-room schoolhouse. Check out the Deer Creek Discovery children's area, which includes a whimsical tree house and water feature. Go south on Wadsworth from C-470, only as far as the stoplight at Deer Creek Canyon Road. Take a right onto Deer Creek Canyon and drive a quarter of a mile. See the gardens on your left at 8500 Deer Creek Canyon Road. *www.botanicgardens.org*

Stretching from the plains across the hogback, **Hildebrand Ranch Park** offers more trail-based recreation in the Chatfield area. The Two-Brands Trail provides a five-mile loop experience when visitors access the hard-surface connector managed by the South Suburban Park and Recreation District. A sister park to Deer Creek Canyon and South Valley Parks, the Hildebrand Ranch Park vi-

sion of a regional amenity continues to be pursued while protecting resources and honoring private property rights. Hildebrand Ranch Park's natural resources include the foothills-shrubland, foothills-meadow, and Ponderosa Pine Savannah communities, and the foothills-canyon riparian communities of Deer Creek and Mill Creek. The environment supports several raptors, prairie dogs, mule deer, elk, bear, mountain lion, and burrowing owls. The Dakota, Lyons, and Niobrara hogbacks are dominant landforms in the park.

In 1866, Frank Hildebrand settled in Deer Creek. Although records about Hildebrand's land acquisition are somewhat contradictory, his ownership was undisputed. Grazing cattle was the predominant activity, with some crops providing winter feed. In 1950, a plan was authorized for a flood-control reservoir in southern Jefferson County to protect Denver, but funds were not appropriated. In 1965, torrential rains on upper Plum Creek brought massive flooding along the

South Platte River, killing 13 and causing millions of dollars in damage. In 1971, the U.S. Secretary of the Army condemned more than 300 acres of the Hildebrand Ranch for Chatfield Reservoir. In 2001, Jefferson County acquired the remaining 1,450 acres of the Hildebrand family holdings for the park. Exit C-470 at Wadsworth Boulevard and head south to the first right turn, Deer Creek Canyon Road. The newly completed trailhead is accessible from Deer Creek Canyon Road approximately 1.3 miles west. *www.jeffco.us*

When first established in 1959, the **Foothills Park & Recreation District** consisted of one park site. The district currently maintains 35 developed neighborhood park sites, three regional parks, eight community parks, 24 greenbelts, 13.5 miles of trails, two public golf course facilities, and 14 reservoirs/ponds and conservation areas totaling more than 3,079 acres of public land. The district boundaries encompass about 28 square miles and serve a population of approximately 90,000 residents. The red rocks of the hogback provide a spectacular backdrop for its geographical boundaries, which generally are Hampden Avenue

on the north, Sheridan Boulevard on the east, and C-470 on the south and west.

Harriman Lake Park features Harriman Lake and the upland prairie habitat surrounding the lake. A 1.4-mile loop trail that surrounds the lake incorporates interpretive stops describing the area's historical and natural features. Improvements at the park have been intentionally limited to preserve the park's natural integrity. From the intersection of South Kipling Parkway and West Quincy Avenue, head south on Kipling to the park entrance and parking lot on the west side of Kipling.

Vehicle access to the parking lot is from southbound Kipling only. *www.ifoothills.org*

While a pool, tennis court, skate park, and playground constitute the main attractions at **Weaver Hollow Park,** the Weaver Gulch Regional Trail begins at Harriman Lake Park and runs through it. From the intersection of South Kipling Parkway and West Quincy Avenue, head west on Quincy two miles to Youngfield Street. Turn left on Youngfield to the park, located on the southeast corner of Youngfield and West Stanford Avenue. A parking lot is available. *www.ifoothills.org*

Boulder County Perhaps no place in America has been as thoughtful or pioneering in protecting open space than Boulder County. In 1967, Boulder County commissioners appointed the first Parks and Open Space Advisory Committee for the County and started an open space department. These two creations resulted in the preservation of thousands of acres of farms through easements and outright purchases. In 1978, Boulder County adopted the Boulder Valley Comprehensive Plan, which guides land use decisions in the County. Open space areas provide the basic structure for the plan because preserving open space protects wildlife habitat, provides opportunities for passive recreation, protects farming and ranching, preserves historic buildings and landscapes, and maintains rural lands between growing communities.

Boulder County started preserving land in the 1970s with funds from voter-approved sales and property taxes. Big ranches were purchased beginning in 1976, including the 775-acre Betasso Preserve west of Boulder and the 2,566-acre Walker Ranch on Flagstaff Road. The first acquisition on the plains occurred in 1979 with the Rock Creek Farm purchase between Lafayette, Louisville, and Broomfield. Since then, the county has preserved about 1,000 properties ranging in size from less than an acre to the 4,923-acre Heil Valley Ranch. To put an acre into perspective, think about the size of a football field. When we add up the acres, Boulder County has preserved approximately 94,000 acres of land, owning 59,000 acres outright and protecting another 35,000 acres via conservation easements. About 40,500 acres of preserved land is located in the foothills and mountains and about 53,500 acres on the plains. *www.bouldercountyopenspace.org*

Boulder

In 1967, City of Boulder voters made history by approving a .4-cent sales tax in perpetuity to buy, manage, and maintain open space—the first time citizens in any U.S. city had voted to tax themselves specifically for open space. The measure passed by a 57 percent majority, an overwhelming demonstration of support in an era of citizen tax concern. Two additional measures that augment the original tax have also been passed. Today, Boulder citizens enjoy more than 45,000 acres of open space land in and around the city. Some of the land is in agricultural production, preserving the historic cultural landscape of Boulder County, while keeping the land open for wildlife and limited recreational uses. In addition to the aesthetic pleasure of Boulder's Open Space & Mountain Parks, an extensive trail system is available for hikers and horseback riders. Bicyclists enjoy riding on designated trails. *www.bouldercolorado.gov*

If you haven't paid a visit to the **Flagstaff Nature Center,** stop by during the summer and fall months. Admission is free. The center is a great place to familiarize yourself with the wildlife, plants, and history of Boulder Open Space and Mountain Parks. Interactive activities and games challenge the child in all of us, and stuffed animal mounts show which species live in the surrounding forests and grasslands. Volunteers are on hand to answer questions about the displays and exhibits. It's open from 10:30 a.m. to 4 p.m. on Saturdays and Sundays, May through September. Located on the summit

of Flagstaff Mountain, the Flagstaff Nature Center can be accessed by following Flagstaff Road approximately 3.5 miles to its junction with Flagstaff Summit Road. Go right on Flagstaff Summit Road and follow it approximately one-half mile to the summit of Flagstaff Mountain. *www.bouldercolorado.gov*

Breathtaking views, quiet solace, inquisitive exploration and vibrant nature, the **Cal-Wood Education Center** is home to all this and more. Nestled in the foothills just outside Jamestown Cal-Wood Education Center offers unique outdoor education experiences to youth and adults alike. In addition, Cal-Wood provides retreats, service-learning, and meeting facilities on their 1,200-acre property. The property is an easy drive from the Boulder-Denver metro area. Once there, you'll find hiking trails, camp sites, cabins, comfortable meeting/retreat rooms in the spacious Calvert Lodge, abundant wildlife and historic features. Cal-Wood was founded in 1982 to realize the vision of Roger and Oral Calvert, who wanted their land to become a place of learning and connecting to the environment. "Education must become the number one priority of the world. We must learn to anticipate, direct and change, and teachers must help students acquire knowledge, ethical standards and lifestyles which recognize our personal responsibility to a quality environment," Roger Calvert once said. Cal-Wood is making that dream a reality by providing workshops for educators to teach environmental education in their classrooms, and offering hands-on, outdoor education programs to youth, especially outreaching to low-income, multi-cultural students. Cal-Wood is about to embark on our first capital campaign to meet the ever-growing demand and serve the larger schools and groups from the Front Range. To learn more about Cal-Wood, visit their website at *www.calwood.org*

Sugarloaf Mountain, a significant natural landmark rising 8,917 feet, is visible from almost any location in the 750 square miles that comprise Boulder County. Mining on and around Sugarloaf Mountain began in 1860 and continued until the 1930s. Since then, Sugarloaf Mountain remains a popular destination for hikers, tourists, and other recreationists. The modest one-mile hike to the summit offers fantastic views. An old mining road—now the trail—ascends from the parking area at the head of Switzerland Trail, a former rail line. On the way down,

Cal-Wood Open Space

Sugarloaf Mountain Open Space

the road switches back through a sparse pine and aspen forest, eventually emerging into the open on the mountain's south side. While on top, linger for a bit to take in the view, and imagine the challenging journeys made by miners on these very roads. Sugarloaf Mountain is 10 miles west of Boulder. From Highway 119/Boulder Canyon, one mile past the tunnel, turn right on Sugarloaf Road. At 4.8 miles, turn right on Sugarloaf Mountain Road. Look east of the lot (which is somewhat of a roundabout with trees in the middle) for the battered metal gate, and start walking on the old road. There's no sign, but the trailhead is one mile up. *www.bouldercountyopenspace.org*

James Walker moved to Boulder in 1869, and he and his wife Phoebe filed a 160-year homestead claim in 1882. The next year, he moved his wife and young son into the newly-built ranch house. Over the next 80 years, the Walker family amassed more than 6,000 acres. When the property was sold in 1959, it was one of the largest cattle ranches in this region of Colorado. Both bait and fly fishing are permitted in South Boulder Creek, which is stocked with rainbow trout. The ranch is north of and contiguous to Eldorado Canyon State Park. From Boulder, drive west on Baseline Road, passing Chautauqua Park and the Flatirons. Baseline Road becomes Flagstaff Road. Continue for 7.5 miles over the top of Flagstaff and behind the backside of Green Mountain. Look for Walker Ranch signs. You can park in the lower parking area or up near the trailhead. *www.bouldercountyopenspace.org*

Eldorado Canyon State Park is a hidden treasure right in Boulder's backyard. Whether you're hiking among the towering sandstone cliffs, picnicking along scenic South Boulder Creek, or climbing Eldo's sheer golden walls, Eldorado Canyon State Park truly has something for everyone. Known for its 500-plus technical rock-climbing routes, Eldorado Canyon lures climbers from around the world. There's also plenty of landscape for hikers, mountain bikers, cross-country skiers, and snowshoers. Picturesque trails vary from easy to difficult, and connect with Boulder trail systems. The quiet beauty of the park can be experienced best in the cooler months, and during summer weekdays. Eldorado Canyon almost always reaches vehicle capacity on weekends and holidays from May through September, and once the park is full, vehicles are only admitted as space becomes available.

The park's riparian habitats serve as movement corridors for mule deer, elk, black bear, bobcat, red fox, coyote, and mountain lion inhabiting the foothills in and around Eldorado Canyon. Large populations of bats breed in the caves in the Inner Canyon; in

With a diverse array of ecosystems, and more than 12 miles of trails—including a single 7.8-mile loop that crosses South Boulder Creek—it's virtually impossible to get bored at **Walker Ranch.** The ranch totals 2,566 acres with an additional 1,212 acres leased from the Bureau of Land Management. The Walker Ranch Homestead consists of original buildings from the 1880s, except for a reconstructed ranch house that replaced the original after it burned to the ground in 1992. The rebuilt ranch house was constructed using environmentally-friendly techniques, while remaining faithful to 1880s architecture, design, and materials. Missourian settler

Eldorado Canyon State Park

fact, seven of the 10 bat species recorded in Boulder County occur in the park. South Boulder Creek supports cold-water fish species, including rainbow, brook, and brown trout, longnose dace, and white and longnose suckers. Over 80 species of migratory and resident birds have been recorded in this area, including raptors, songbirds, and waterfowl. Golden eagles, red-tailed hawks, and prairie falcons nest within and around the park, and seasonal closures of some climbing routes are enforced to protect raptor nesting sites. Sightings of wild turkeys and blue grouse occur in Crescent Meadows and American dippers may be seen along streams. Eldorado Canyon State Park is located about five miles southwest of Boulder. From Boulder, take Broadway/Highway 93 south. Turn west onto Highway 170 and continue about three miles to the town of Eldorado Springs. Highway 170 dead-ends at the town, and a dirt road continues to the park on your left. *www.parks.state.co.us*

While the majority of wetlands in the Boulder Valley are less than 10 acres, **Sombrero Marsh** totals more than 20, making it an exceptional ecological resource. The soils, hydrology, and vegetation in this naturally-occurring wetland create important habitat for many birds, mammals, amphibians, and invertebrates. The marsh's brackish waters and seasonal salt flats support uncommon wetland plant communities.

The Sombrero Marsh Partnership—between Boulder's Open Space and Mountain Parks Department, the Boulder Valley School District, and Thorne Ecological Institute—strives to restore and sustain the marsh's ecological health and function. This unique partnership resulted in the Sombrero Marsh Environmental Education Center, which promotes ecological literacy among Boulder Valley students by providing education that supports the school district's curriculum. The marsh provides a rich setting for teaching children and adults about wetland ecology, environmental restoration, and the necessity for land stewardship.

Two designated conservation areas—closed to the public year-round—protect the ranch's important wildlife, plants, and cultural resources. Although moose, elk, trout, bats, amphibians, and breeding birds are monitored here, other wildlife live within or pass through the area, including black bears, mule deer, mountain lions, coyotes, bobcats, beavers, and short-tailed weasels. In addition, nearly 90 species of birds have been spotted at Caribou Ranch, and many amphibians

and reptiles reside here. Trees are also abundant. See if you can tell the difference between the pines, firs, and spruces, and be on the lookout for golden aspen in fall. Due to its altitude, many of the ranch's wildflowers bloom later in the year than those at other Boulder County Parks and Open Space properties.

Rock 'n' roll aficionados may recall the Caribou Ranch recording studio. A barn until 1971, the studio was situated on private property near the open space. Caribou Ranch studio attracted major artists, including U2, Billy Joel, Chicago, Elton John, Rod Stewart, the late Dan Fogelberg, and many others. The studio closed after a fire destroyed the control room in 1985.

The ranch's parking lot can fit 25 vehicles and one school bus. Horse trailer parking is available at Mud Lake parking lot, three-quarters of a mile east of the main lot with a connecting trail to Caribou Ranch. Bicycles and dogs are not permitted, and Caribou Ranch is closed annually from April 1 through June 30 to protect spring migratory birds, and elk calving and rearing. The park re-opens on July 1. Caribou Ranch is located two miles north of Nederland. Turn west on County Road 126 from the Peak to Peak Scenic Byway/Highway 72, and follow it to the parking lot on the right. *www.bouldercountyopenspace.org*

Nederland Ice and Racquet Park boasts an Olympic-size outdoor ice rink in winter and three regulation-size, double tennis courts in the warmer months. Located in Nederland's Indian Peaks subdivision, the 180-feet-by-80-feet sheet of open-air ice is natural (unrefrigerated), so be prepared for all kinds of ice conditions, including snow. Features include small warming huts, lighted night skating, a full schedule of activities, and plenty of fresh mountain air. The volunteer-run ice rink, typically open from December through February, transitions into three regulation-sized, double tennis courts from May through October. Both lessons and open skating/playing are available, and fees are nominal. The full-

sized venue is partially built into the hillside, providing protection from the wind for skaters and shade for the ice—ideal for maintaining prime skating conditions. If you're looking for a true mountain skating experience, this is it: The entire property is heavily forested, providing a picturesque setting. From the Nederland traffic circle, go north on Highway 72/Peak to Peak toward Estes Park. Travel up a hill past the Nederland Community Center on your right. After 0.8 of a mile, turn left on Indian Peaks Drive. You'll see the Elementary School road sign. Continue straight on Indian Peaks Drive, ignoring the sharp left at School Road. Just past another left at Shoshoni Way, the paved road turns to dirt. Continue another 200 feet to the park on your left. *www.nedrink.org*

Beautiful Nederland also provides the **Nathan Lazarus Skate Park,** one of best skate park settings in Colorado. Features include a pool, flow bowl, cradle, hoodie, and wall ride with tombstone mini-bowl.

Find it south of Highway 119 on East 1st Street, next to Barker Meadow Reservoir. *www.nathanlazarusskatepark.com*

Lyons

With beautiful hanging valleys, picturesque vistas, and forests, **Heil Valley Ranch** is a playground for wildlife—and people. One visit to this 5,020-acre property could turn anyone into an outdoor enthusiast. With the highest species diversity of any Boulder County Parks and Open Space property, Heil Valley Ranch is an excellent place to view wildlife. Nearly 100 bird species have been observed in one season, including golden eagles, prairie falcons, violet-green swallows, woodpeckers, hummingbirds, and chickadees. Seventy percent of all mammal species found in Boulder County can be found here, including Abert's squirrels, cottontail rabbits, prairie dogs, marmots, red and gray foxes, mule deer, bobcats, black bears, and mountain lions.

Heil-Lyons Connector Trail, aka **Picture Rock Trail,** is one of five trails in Heil Valley Ranch. The 5.2-mile Picture Rock Trail connects Heil Ranch with the town of Lyons, and affords views of the defunct Whitestone and Vickery Quarry complex, a significant quarry operation from the 1890s to the 1960s. Lyons sandstone was mined there and used to build the University of Colorado's Boulder campus. You'll also see the remains of the Whitestone ranch, including a sand-

Heil Valley Ranch

stone loafing shed, ranch house, well, and silo. Although Picture Rock got its name from the colorful patterns stained into the rock's surface through the quarrying process, none of the patterned rock remains today. You will, however, catch views of red sandstone mesas as you gain elevation. The unique patterns and color of the stone are results of Colorado's freeze-thaw cycle. Picture Rock Trail is well maintained with plenty of signage, and the easy elevation gain makes for an enjoyable hike or bike. The ranch is 2.5 miles south of Lyons, just west of Highway 36. The Lyons trailhead is located at the end of Red Gulch Road. From Lyons, go south on Highway 7. Take a left onto Old St. Vrain Road and another left on Red Gulch Road. The trailhead and parking are on the left. *www.bouldercountyopenspace.org*

The **Lyons Whitewater Park** in Meadow Park is frequented by kayakers, tubers, and fishing enthusiasts. Comprising a quarter-mile-long stretch of North St. Vrain Creek, the water park contains a series of beginning-to-intermediate drop structures, including the Black Bear and October holes. Starting near the "swimming hole," the Lyons Whitewater Park bends around the west end of Meadow Park, making it an easy walk for kayakers and tubers from the last take-out back to the start. The park is just west of 5th Avenue/Highway 7 at the end of Park Drive.

a hotel, tavern, and stage station for the Overland Mail Stage route. In 1888, owner Mary Miller founded the town of Lafayette, naming it after her husband Lafayette Miller. Head south on 104th Street from Dillon Road and under the Northwest Parkway. It's a little less than a mile to the trailhead at Stearns Lake. The Rock Creek Trail, which is open to pedestrians, cyclists, and equestrians, is continuous from 120th Street in Lafayette, through Rock Creek Farm, past Stearns Lake and up to Brainard Drive in Broomfield. *www.bouldercountyopenspace.org*

Greenlee Wildlife Preserve is a 13-acre sanctuary that is home to a variety of birds, mammals, amphibians, insects, and native plants. Greenlee provides sanctuary for wildlife intolerant of the human activity at Waneka Lake; protects native plants and vegetation valuable to wildlife; links habitat areas used by wildlife moving through the region; and serves as an environmental education site for schools. Use one of Waneka Park's two entrances: The east entrance, at 705 Caria Drive, is easily accessed from Baseline Road by turn-

ing south o[...]
from Public[...]
entrance, at[...]
turning nor[...]
Centaur V[...]
Drive. Follo[...]
to the park[...]
serve can be[...]
dirt Waneka[...]
circles the l[...]

The **Lafaye[...]
to the Bob[...]
the in-line[...]
Road at the[...]
and West D[...]

Sandstone Ranch Park

picnic ta
ters. Park
Austin A

Lafaye
A calmi
area, **Ca**
Creek F
and Lafa
accessib
dog wal
mounta
lowed a
large an
Shorebi
wading
species
migratio
phibian
also ma
Stearns
read the
Rock C

Carolyn Holmberg Preserve at Rock Creek Farm

Cheyenne Mountain State Park

COLORADO SPRINGS AREA

El Paso County

106

COLORADO SPRINGS AREA

El Paso County

116

10

Front Range foothills e...
acre preserve is compri...
types, including shrubla...
meadows, pinyon-junip...
mixed coniferous wood...
like Cheyenne Mountain...
no development. Approp...
ornithologist Charles Aike...
ideal destination for birde...
species have been spotted...
veyor, taxidermist, and co...
surveyed this region in the...
versity of plant and anir...
thrive in Aiken Canyon, w...
the zone between the plain...
where dramatic red spires a...
lide with rich green flora. ...
can be found—and made—...

Bluestem Prairie Open Space

Bluestem Prairie Open Space wraps around much of the Big Johnson Reservoir, which sits adjacent to the Colorado Springs Airport. In addition to its spectacular views of the Front Range and Pikes Peak to the west and grasslands to the east, Bluestem Prairie is special because of its vegetation and wildlife. The property is dominated by a mixed- grass prairie composed of grasses that include blue grama, buffalograss, sideoats grama, big bluestem, little bluestem, sleepygrass, and green needlegrass. Also a bird watcher's paradise, Bluestem is a wintering area for the federally threatened bald eagle according to the Colorado Natural Heritage Program, and hosts numerous other bird species. While birding, you're likely to encounter pronghorn antelope, tiger salamanders, black-tailed prairie dogs, and voles. From Colorado Springs, take I-25 south to exit 138. Turn east onto Lake Avenue, which turns into South Circle Drive. Turn south onto Hancock Road, which becomes Hancock Expressway. Turn east on Drennan Road, and then south onto Powers Boulevard. You'll see the open space after 1.5 miles. *www.palmer landtrust.org* and *www.springsgov.com*

Manitou Springs

Red Mountain Trail is one mile and takes you to the top of Red Mountain (altitude 7,375 feet), a small mountain on the southern edge of Manitou Springs. The ascent is moderate with the view from the top making this a popular hiking destination. In Manitou Springs, turn south on Pawnee from Manitou Avenue, and travel all the way up the residential road. Eventually, Pawnee becomes a dirt road. You'll see the trailhead for the Intenmann Trail on the right. Hike on the Intenmann Trail for approximately .4 miles, and turn left at the clearly-marked sign for Red Mountain.

Red Rock Canyon Open Space is a 787-acre property located between Colorado Springs and Manitou Springs. Palmer Land Trust holds a conservation easement that protects approximately 652 acres of the property from ever being developed. The majority of Red Rock Canyon remains in a natural state, offering unique opportunities to view geologic formations, natural plant communities, wildlife, and impressive vistas of the surrounding foothills, including marvelous views

Red Rock Canyon Open Space

of Garden of the Gods. I've made some of my best red rock photography here—as good as places I've photographed in the canyon country of Western Colorado and around Moab, Utah!

The property is rich in historical, archeological, and cultural value. Artifacts found here are evidence of the many prehistoric cultures that frequented the area. Visible mining, quarrying, and homesteading activity throughout the open space are indicative of more recent history. An important public resource, Red Rock Canyon provides a number of educational and recreational opportunities. Through interpretive signs, markers, and kiosks, you can learn about the unique geological features, cultural and historical significance, and biological resources of this amazing piece of property. An extensive trail network gives hikers and mountain bikers of all skill levels abundant opportunities to explore. The open space is located along Highway 24. From I-25, take Exit Highway 24/Cimarron Street west. After the 31st Street light, turn left onto Ridge Road. Red Rock Canyon is on the south side of the street with the parking lot at the end of Ridge Road. *www.redrockcanyonopenspace.org*

Fountain

The **Fountain Creek Regional Trail** begins where the Pikes Peak Greenway ends, and follows Fountain Creek from the Janitell Bridge in southern Colorado Springs through Fountain Creek Regional Park. Hikers, bikers, and horseback riders enjoy a variety of wildlife attracted to the water's edge along the ribbon of large cottonwoods, which line this riparian corridor.

Fountain Creek Regional Park (and two adjacent private parcels) is located between the towns of Widefield and Fountain, north of the Colorado Springs State Wildlife Area and east of Fort Carson. The site contains five distinct natural communities: creek, cottonwood/willow woodlands, meadow, marsh, and pond. Fountain Creek and a series of spring-fed ponds run through the park, which encompasses approximately 25 acres and is fenced on all sides. Dogs love to splash around in Bear Creek, which runs along the park's south side. From I-25, take the Security-Widefield Exit/Highway 16 east to Highway 85. Go south one mile to Duckwood Street. Turn right into the parking lot. *http://adm.elpasoco.com*

Fountain Creek Regional Trail

A 50-acre wetland preserve along Fountain Creek, **Adams Open Space** features a lovely trail through meadows and stately deciduous trees. Main Street in Fountain turns into Old Pueblo Road as you drive south. The preserve is on the left about one mile south of town. A Colorado Opens Lands sign marks the property.

Calhan

Explore the colorful clay and stone spires called hoodoos at the **Paint Mines Interpretive Park** near Calhan. There's nothing else quite like this in Colorado, and the photographs can be equally unique. The rocks can be quite bright in daylight, so try photographing them on a cloudy day, or at sunrise and sunset. I love images of the rocks decorated with snow. A network of trails covering 4.5 miles guides you through the prairie, hoodoos, and streams in the 750-acre park named for the early American Indians who made their paints and decorated ceremonial pottery on this site. The Indians also used the petrified wood nearby to fashion dart and arrow points. In the 1800s, Euro-Americans settled in the region for agriculture and ranching, and used the clay to make bricks. Take Highway 24 east from Colorado Springs to Calhan. Turn south on Yoder Road/Calhan Highway, and drive about a mile to Paint Mines Road. Turn east on Paint Mines Road, and drive about 1.5 miles to the first designated parking area. The park includes restrooms, and has signs throughout the trail system explaining the geology and ecology of the area. Open seven days a week from dawn till dusk. *http://adm.elpasoco.com*

and other wildlife spe tures, Muel lovers. Mor resident bir ted raptors hawk, Co kestrel, gre Visitors als bird, comn hairy woo

Eastern Plains

Divide

An amaz
acres mal
enthusias
season, y
on foot, s
tain bike
the backs
wildflowe
watching
bears, ha

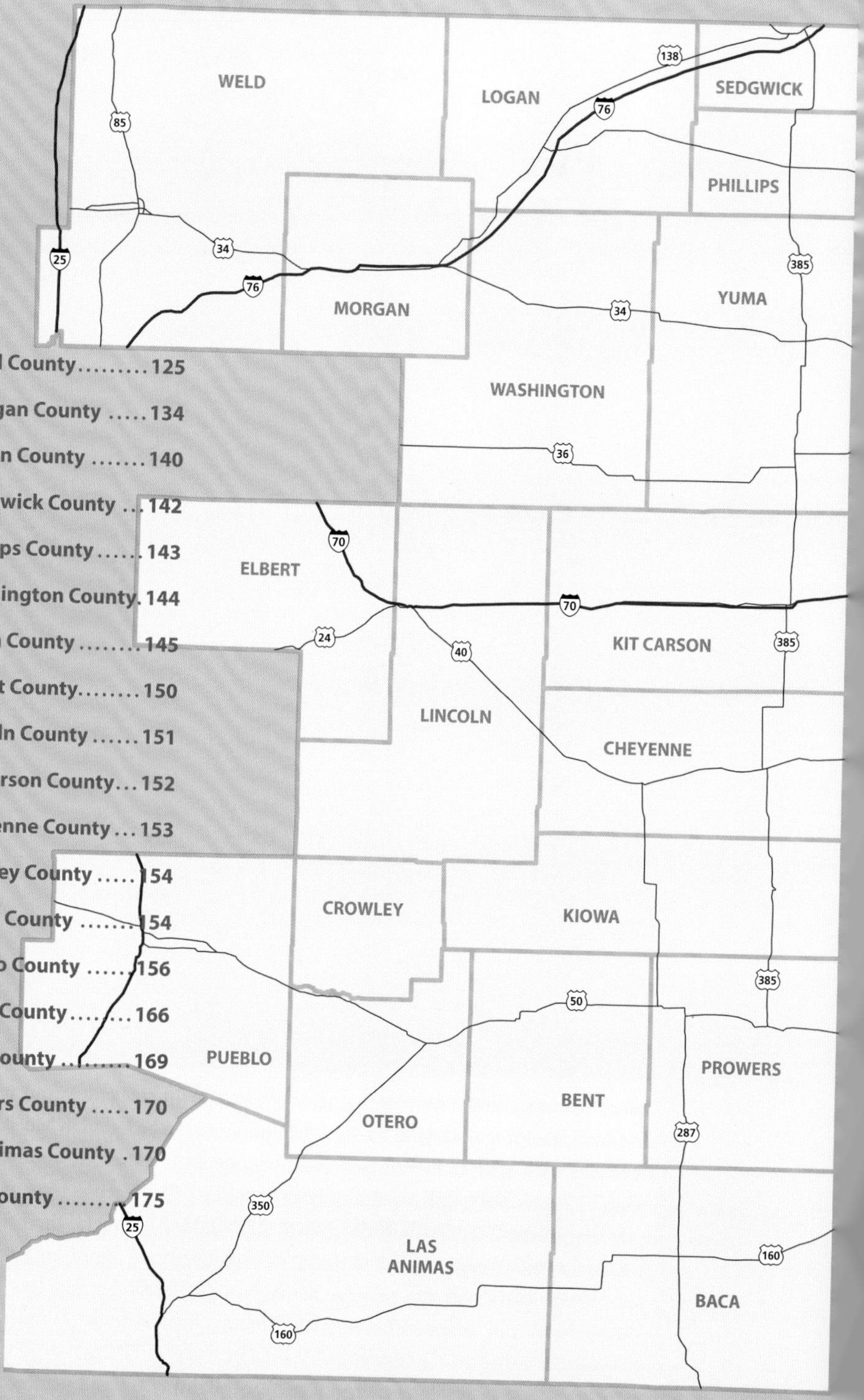

Eastern Plains

Though the views are somewhat less dramatic without snowcapped peaks in the background (although these are visible in many counties), the riparian areas, reservoirs, rivers, smells, sounds, and wildlife-viewing opportunities found in Colorado's Eastern Plains are no less sublime! I love waking up to views of yellow, orange, and red layers of clouds capping a prairie landscape. Dwellings, barns, and old fences—remains of Dust Bowl days during the Great Depression—are seen everywhere, evoking a sense of history like their mountain counterparts, the mining camps. Modern gleaming-silver grain silos are the perfect complement to the past. Remarkable photo opps exist in the Eastern Plains: Look for fields of wheat and other crops, cows grazing in meadows, and cottonwood trees decorating dry creek beds. Tiny agrarian towns dot the plains, each with its own idyllic park, playground, and trail for residents and visitors alike. More diverse recreational opportunities are available closer to the Front Range mountains and the larger communities of Weld, Pueblo, and Las Animas Counties.

Weld County

Currently under construction, the 20-mile Poudre River Trail will extend from Island Grove Regional Park in Greeley west to the Weld/Larimer County line along the beautiful Cache la Poudre River. The trail is being built through a cooperative effort between the cities of Greeley and Windsor, and Weld County. Several contiguous sections are complete. The trail offers non-motorized recreational opportunities such as biking, walking, running, and rollerblading. Take a break to visit historical and educational sites along the trail.

While certain details are up for debate, according to some historical accounts, the Cache la Poudre River's name derives from an incident involving a party of French trappers traveling along the banks of the river in the 1800s. The men were caught in a snowstorm and buried their gunpowder in a cache near the river. The Poudre's headwaters are in magnificent Rocky Mountain National Park. Since the beginning of the western settlement of Northern Colorado, this river has become the lifeblood of the area and one of the state's most important natural resources. It provides a source of water for agriculture and residents, a habitat and refuge for wildlife, and unlimited possibilities for recreation. Although the

river appears quite different today than it did 100 years ago—it resembles only a stream in some locations during winter months—the Poudre Trail allows people to experience the beauty of the river while also preserving the river's edge and the habitat for the wildlife living near the river. To get to Island Grove Regional Park Trailhead from I-25, take the Highway 34/Greeley Exit, and go east to 35th Avenue. Turn north and go to 10th Street. Turn east and go to 14th Avenue. Turn north and follow 14th Avenue into Island Grove Regional Park. Visit *www.poudretrail.org* for trailheads the sections of the trail that are currently open.

St. Vrain State Park offers 604 acres of land and 152 acres of water split among 14 ponds (formerly called Barbour Ponds). St. Vrain Creek forms its northern boundary. While it's a great place for anglers, campers, photographers, walkers, and anyone who loves nature, bird lovers are particularly drawn to the park for its diversity of bird species. St. Vrain is not only home to the largest heron rookery in the state, but it's also the only known nesting site of great egrets in Colorado. In addition, the park provides winter habitat for bald eagles and summer habitat for American white pel-

Poudre River Trail

icans, both of which are species of concern in Colorado. Birds of prey such as red-tailed hawks and osprey nest in the park, and many waterfowl species, songbirds, and shorebirds choose St. Vrain as their nesting site. Four miles of trails will get you to the various ponds. Fishing piers are available for avid fishing enthusiasts, but beware of the many muskrats that like to try stealing your fish! Bass, crappie, blue gill, yellow perch, pumpkinseed, rainbow trout, carp, and catfish are among the many fish species found here. Take Exit 240 from I-25 onto Colorado 119 west, then travel north on County Road 7 until it ends at County Road 24 1/2. Turn right to the park entrance. *www.parks.state.co.us*

The 1,195 acres at **Centennial Valley State Wildlife Area** provide plenty of ground for hunting waterfowl, deer, small game, and turkey, as well as for wildlife viewing. From Greeley, go 14 miles east on Highway 34 to County Road 50, then 1.5 miles east to County Road 380 and the parking area. *www.wildlife.state.co.us*

Centennial Valley State Wildlife Area

Berthoud

Hillsdale Park is an 11-acre park located within the Dry Creek flood plain. This beautiful park has a walking trail offering a close-up view of nature unlike any other in the area. From I-25 north of Longmont, take Highway 56 west through Berthoud to County Road 17. Go south to Spartan Avenue. Turn east and go to South 9th Street to the park. *www.berthoud.org*

Evans

One of the newer parks in Evans, **Prairie View Park** features a picnic pavilion, basketball court, playground, soccer field, restrooms, and the town's first skate park. From I-25, head east on Highway 34 (as if going to Greeley) to 35th Avenue. Go south to Prairie View Drive/42nd Street, then east to Harbor Lane. Turn north to the park at Prairie View Drive and Harbor Lane. *www.cityofevans.org*

Firestone

Harney Park is a small local park in the Saint Vrain Ranch Park West subdivision. From I-25, take the Highway 119 Exit eastbound/County Road 24 to Colorado Boulevard. Head south to County Road 22, then east to the first left, Devonshire Street. Follow it to the park on the left. **Firestone Regional Sports Complex** has all the ball fields a community could possibly want, but its claim to fame could be its playground. With a total of 2,489 pieces and parts, it's certainly the largest in the community—and the most colorful. The playground boasts a giant ladybug, bongo pod, hippo slide, gravity cube, and jax web, as well as spring riders and toddler chimes. Located at the southwest corner of County Roads 24 and 115/Frontier Street. *www.ci.firestone.co.us*

Harney Park

University of Northern Colorado Xeriscape Garden

Frederick

The 129-acre **Frederick Recreation Area** surrounds Milavec Reservoir, which provides fishing and non-motorized boating opportunities, and attracts an interesting collection of wildlife including deer, coyotes, bald eagles, American pelican, and snapping turtles. A six-foot-wide, ADA-accessible concrete walk connects the park to the St. Vrain Legacy Trail. Other park features include a playground, picnic area, pavilion, basketball court, dog park, and a running trail around the lake. The area is on the northwest corner of the intersection of Colorado Boulevard/County Road 13 and Godding Hollow Parkway/County Road 18 west of the Safeway Marketplace. *www.frederickco.gov*

Greeley

Wildlife gardening and landscape water conservation are on display at the **University of Northern Colorado Xeriscape Garden,** which entails several community xeric demonstration gardens. Incorporating the basic elements of food, water, and cover needed to attract urban wildlife, the project design features low-maintenance plants that require minimal water and create habitat for wildlife. Informative park signage details the practice of xeriscaping and gardening for wildlife. The gardens allow individuals, clubs, or organizations to conduct field research, testing, and display of materials, plants, or methods promoting water-wise gardening. Garden plots here are available for rental by Greely residents. From 23rd Avenue in Greeley, go east on Reservoir Road to 17th Avenue on the northwest corner of the campus. *www.greeleygov.com*

Missile Site Park offers a unique opportunity to step back into the Cold War Era of national defense. One of four Atlas E sites in Colorado, the park contains a replica of Atlas E, a

nuclear warhead-equipped missile constructed in 1961 and deactivated in 1965 as well as historical information and artifacts. The host military base for the Atlas E program's command and control was located at Francis E. Warren Air Force Base in Cheyenne, Wyoming. After deactivation, the Atlas E site was turned over to Weld County. Missile Site Park's caretaker lives on site, and is able to assist with campground activities and tours. Take the Highway 34/Greeley Exit east from I-25, and follow the Highway 257/34 left-hand fork. After turning left on the 257 Spur Road, follow signs to the park. *www.co.weld.co.us/Departments/BuildingsandGrounds/MissileSitePark.html*

Johnstown

The **Outdoor Classroom at Civic Park** includes displays and information on wildlife and plants native to Weld County. It's located behind Glenn A. Jones M.D. Memorial Library at 400 South Parish Avenue. *www.townofjohnstown.com*

Milliken

Sappington Park offers trails, trees, and a large open space. Accommodating folks of all ages, the park plays host to Milliken's annual Easter Eggstravaganza. Knowledge Quest Academy students also put the large area to use during recess and physical education activities. From I-25, take Highway 60/Johnstown Exit east through Johnstown to Milliken's Broad Street. Proceed past Alice Avenue to Traders Lane on the right. Go south to Village Drive, left to Schoolhouse Drive, and left to the park. *www.millikenco.gov*

Outdoor Classroom at Civic Park

Eastman Park Skate Park

Boardwalk Community Park

Chimney Park

Diamond Valley Community Park and Sports Complex

Windsor

The town of Windsor has cool local parks to visit on hot summer days. A healthy 25 acres, **Eastman Park** contains a pond, playground, athletic fields, and the **Eastman Park Skate Park.** The Poudre River Trail passes through, too. Take the Highway 392/Windsor Exit from I-25, and go east to CR-17/7th Street. Go south to Eastman Park Drive, and look for the park on the right. **Boardwalk Community Park** is a 12-acre park featuring a natural amphitheater, great playground, the Town of Windsor Museums, and Windsor Lake and its contiguous trail. Once again, take the I-25 Windsor Exit to 7th Street, but this time turn north. Make a right on Birch Street to the park. The 17-acre **Chimney Park** offers a pool with locker rooms and restrooms, a playground, and athletic fields. Continue through Windsor on Highway 392/Main Street to 1st Street. Go south to Chestnut Street and east to the park on your left. **Diamond Valley Community Park and Sports Complex** consists of 85 acres and currently contains three softball fields with more amenities to come. From Eastman Park, continue east on Eastman Park Drive past County Road 19 to the park on the left. Map available at *www.ci.windsor.co.us.*

Morgan County

Fort Morgan

A beautiful trail runs for more than a mile along the South Platte River through and beyond **Riverside Park**. This is a great place to access and photograph the river once known as being "a mile wide and an inch deep." Park features include a swimming pool, playground, inline skate rink, ball fields, and the Rainbow Arch Bridge, built in 1923 and considered an architectural gem. Spanning 1,100 feet, this arch bridge is among the longest in the nation and the only one of its kind in Colorado. The bridge makes a striking entrance to the Pawnee Pioneer Trails Scenic Byway, which takes visitors through the Pawnee National Grassland, a natural prairie that has changed little since pioneers passed through it in covered wagons via the Overland Trail. From I-76, head north at the main Fort Morgan Exit on Highway 52. The park and the bridge are on the right before the river.

Fulton Heights Playground is a community park at 301 Aurora Street. From Highway 52, go west on Highway 34/Platte Avenue, then south on West Street to Kiowa Avenue, then west to the park. *www.cityoffortmorgan.com*

Riverside Park

High Plains Park

Wiggins

Fourteen miles east of Fort Morgan on the south side of I-76, you'll find the town of Wiggins and **High Plains Park** featuring a playground and a skate park. Take Exit 64 from I-76, and head east on Central Avenue. The skate park is on your right.

The 2,571-acre **Elliott State Wildlife Area** features hunting, hiking, and plenty of wildlife. Deer, rabbit, squirrel, pheasant, bobwhite quail, dove, and waterfowl are frequently hunted here, although access might be limited at various times of the year. One of the most frequently birded counties in Colorado's Eastern Plains, Morgan County features habitats typical of the High Plains ecosystem: shortgrass prairie, sandhills scrub, irrigated agriculture (mostly hay fields), riparian areas along the South Platte River and related irrigation reservoirs, and managed landscapes of

Elliott State Wildlife Area

homesteads. Take I-76 Exit 90B, and go north on Highway 71 for 1.5 miles to a junction with County Road 28. Continue east on 71 for six miles to Snyder. This wildlife area consists of three sections, all along County Road W7: The North and South Hamlin tracts are five miles northeast of Snyder, the Union Tract is one mile further northeast, and the Elliott and Quint Tracts just north of that one. For maps and regulations, visit *www.wildlife.state.co.us.*

Located adjacent to Jackson Lake State Park in western Morgan County, the 710-acre **Andrick Ponds State Wildlife Area** features picturesque rolling topography with mixed groundcover that includes open water, wetland vegetation, grassland, sand sage, and open woodland. An extensive network of individual water bodies exists on the property, ranging from small potholes to a 25-acre lake. Well known for supplying Northeast Colorado with large numbers of duck, geese, and other quality waterfowl hunting, the property also offers prime habitat for small game, turkeys, deer, and bald eagles. From Interstate 76 at the Highway 39 exit (Exit 66), go 7.4 miles north on Highway 39 to Highway 144 and Morgan County Road Y.5, then 1.5 miles west on Morgan County Road Y.5. Turn north on Morgan County Road 3 for 1.5 miles to Morgan County Road AA. Go west on Morgan County Road AA just before the entrance to Jackson Lake State Park and go 1 mile to Morgan County Road 2. Turn south on Morgan County Road 2 for .54 miles to the parking entrance and parking area on the east side of Morgan County Road 2. To access the south parking lot, continue south on Morgan County Road 2 one-half mile to the parking lot on the east side. Visit *www.wildlife.state. co.us* for maps and regulations.

Jackson Lake at **Jackson Lake State Park** is ranked one of the "Top 15 Park Beaches" by Reserve America. Also popular with birders and hunters, the state park is located in the central flyway for migratory birds. In fact, the abundance and diversity of bird species draws

Jackson Lake State Park

birders from throughout the region. Ferruginous and rough-legged hawks are present in the winter, and Swainson's hawks return for the summer months. The warmer weather also brings large numbers of American white pelicans to Jackson Lake. Long-billed curlews and whooping cranes are observed on occasion, and you might be lucky enough to spot a northern harrier flying low over the park's wetlands and grasslands. Ground-nesting grassland birds, including horned larks, lark buntings, western meadowlarks and vesper sparrows, are known to sometimes breed here in the spring. In the winter, awe-inspiring bald eagles can be seen perched in cottonwoods or soaring over the reservoir.

Jackson Lake is stocked with northern pike and large and small-mouth bass, as well as warm-water fish such as walleye, saugeye, catfish, perch, rainbow trout, crappie, and wipers. Wildlife watchers visiting the park might come across white-tailed or mule deer, coyote, red fox, cottontail rabbit, black-tailed jackrabbit, fox squirrel or thirteen-lined ground squirrel. Trails at Jackson Lake include the Prairie Wetland Nature Trail, a one-quarter-mile, self-guided trail located north of Cove Campground; a 1.5-mile trail located between the visitor center and Northview Campground; and a trail on the south side of the park that runs from the south swim beach to the Cottonwood picnic area. Folks also enjoy walking along the shoreline or along park roadways. Abundant photo opportunities exist here— sunrise is especially beautiful to capture! Jackson Lake has 260 campsites most of which can accommodate campers, trailers, or tents. Facilities include showers, toilets, laundry, electric hook-ups, and drinking water.

From I-76, take Exit 66 (the second Wiggins exit). Turn left on Highway 39/52 and travel approximately nine miles. Go one-half mile past Goodrich to the T-intersection and turn left onto County Road Y5, which turns north after a couple of miles. This will take you past the south side of the park and into the main area on the west. *www.parks.state.co.us*

Logan County
Sterling

When heading northeast on I-76, stop off in Sterling to cool off under the cottonwood trees or for a leisurely walk on the beautiful .7-mile walking/biking and fitness trail that winds around **Columbine Park**. Accessible for people with wheelchairs, the park has a picnic area, restrooms, and other facilities. Located on Sterling's south side, the park is on the east

Columbine Park

Pioneer Park

Prairie Park

side of Highway 6 at South Division Avenue. **Pioneer Park** offers 1.4 miles of trails, and is located two miles west of Sterling at Highway 14/Main Street and County Road 37/Beal Road. Sterling's newest park, **Prairie Park** is located south of the Sterling Recreation Center between Broadway and Elm Streets, and has many amenities. *www.sterlingcolo.com*

I love photographing sunrises and sunsets along the South Platte River. Its slow-moving waters make for great reflections of pink skies. Your best bet for such a photo is to stand on one of the many bridges crossing the river along the I-76 corridor, but you can also get this shot on various public lands. **Bravo State Wildlife Area,** northeast of Sterling, lies right on the river. With hunting for deer, rabbit, squirrel, bobwhite quail, pheasant, turkey, dove, and waterfowl, it offers splendid bird and wildlife viewing opportunities. From I-76, take Exit 125 at Sterling. Go one-half mile west on Highway 14 to County Road 370, then northeast two miles

to the first parking area. Travel two miles farther on 370 to reach the second parking area on the left. **Overland Trail State Wildlife Area** is south of Sterling on the river at Atwood. From I-76, take Exit 115/Atwood, and go 2.5 miles north on Highway 63 to County Road 16. Then, go one-half mile east to the sign and access road on the left. *www.wildlife.state.co.us*

Overland Trail State Wildlife Area

Bravo State Wildlife Area

Fleming

Fleming is a 100-year-old plains community located 19 miles east of Sterling on Highway 6. If you're heading toward the sand hills of Nebraska, stop for a break at Fleming's **North Park** where you'll find a great playground and skate park. It's in front of the Fleming School on North Fremont Avenue. *www.neco-land.com*

Sedgwick County

Located in the extreme northeast corner of Colorado just beyond the crossroads of I-80 and I-76, Sedgwick County is bound to the north and east by Nebraska. As an entry point into the state, the county is often referred to as the "Gateway to Colorado." The climate, growing season, precipitation, surface and ground water, soil characteristics, and natural vegetation make the area conducive to farm and ranch production. Sedgwick County depends on various types of agricultural production as its economic base including wheat, barley, grain sugar beets, and cattle. *www.northeastcoloradotourism.com*

Julesburg

Julesburg has four parks and a community pool located at 9th and Oak Streets. **Union Pacific Railroad Park,** located at Cedar and First Streets, has a beautiful gazebo and lots of shade trees. If you're a railway enthusiast, it's the perfect place to spend an afternoon watching the trains go by. *http://townofjulesburg.com*

Phillips County

One of the most productive farming and ranching regions in our country, Phillips County is located on the beautiful High Plains of Northeastern Colorado. The excellent dryland and irrigated cropland here produce wheat, corn, beans, popcorn, and alfalfa. You'll also find several fine livestock and feedlot operations. *www.northeastcoloradotourism.com*

Holyoke Municipal Park and Pool

Golden Plains Recreation Center

Haxton

Eighteen miles east of Holyoke on Highway 6 is the agrarian town of Haxton and the **Bullpup Playground** in Haxton's municipal park. Go north on Washington Street to Grant Street, and head east to the park. *www.northeastcoloradotourism.com*

Holyoke

No need to overheat in the summer in Northeastern Colorado. Cool off picnicking under the stately trees or in the pool at **Holyoke Municipal Park and Pool.** From Highway 6, head south on Highway 385/Interocean Avenue to the park at 248 East Kellogg Street. Need a workout? Visit the **Golden Plains Recreation Center** at 212 South Interocean Avenue. *www.northeastcoloradotourism.com*

Bullpup Playground

Washington County
Akron

This small town boasts a great skate park in **Akron Swimming Pool Park,** located at Elm and 4th Streets.

Featuring fine bird and wildlife viewing on the South Platte River, **Messex State Wildlife Area** is located south of the town of Merino a few miles north of I-76. Fall color peaks here in October. From I-76, take either Exit 102/Merino or Exit 115/Highway 63 and head north to Highway 6. If you choose the first option, travel northeast on Highway 6; if you choose the second, travel southwest to County Road 6 (7.5 miles from the Merino exit). Head west along CR 6 for about 2.5 miles, and the northern parking lot will be on your left. To get to the southern unit of Messex SWA, take CR 6 a couple of miles further to County Road 15.5, and turn left. Follow this road for two miles, and then turn left onto County Road 59. After about a mile, you'll cross the river and see the SWA. *www.wildlife.state.co.us*

Messex State Wildlife Area

Wray Rainbow Park and Municipal Pool

Yuma County

Wray

Wray sits along the banks of the Republican River's north fork near the Nebraska-Colorado border. It gets hot in the summer among the sand hills of Yuma County, so cool off at the **Wray Rainbow Park and Municipal Pool**. From Highway 385 in Wray, head west on Highway 34/3rd Street to Jackson Street. Go south on Jackson to the park on your left. **Wray Community Activity Park** features a lovely garden and landscaping. Located on Highway 34/3rd Street, on the left, just a short distance east of Highway 385. *www.wrayco.net*

Eckley Community Park and Skate Park

West of Wray lies the town of Eckley and the **Eckley Community Park and Skate Park**. Take Main Street north from Highway 34 to Hendricks Street. Head east to the park.

Yuma City Park

West of Eckley is the town of Yuma and the **Yuma City Park.** Head north from Highway 34 on Main Street to 2nd Avenue. Turn west to the park.

South of Wray is the town of Idalia and the **Idalia Visions Playground.** Find it at the school by heading north on Richards Street from Highway 36.

West of Idalia is the tiny town of Joes. Check out the **Prairie Walk and Park** located on the north side of Highway 36.

Bonny Lake State Park and **South Republican State Wildlife Area** provide bird and

Prairie Walk and Park

South Republican State Wildlife Area

wildlife viewing along the Republican River's south fork in southern Yuma County. Wildlife in the area range from deer to bald eagles and many other birds, and diverse wetland, riparian, and aquatic plant communities exist in both locations. Bonny Lake State Park was decommissioned in 2011 due to Colorado Division of Parks and Wildlife budget constraints. However, you can still drive through the park on the way to the State Wildlife Area to the east.

Bonny Prairie Natural Area offers a remnant of the little blue stem loess prairie that once covered thousands of square miles in Colorado, Kansas, and Nebraska. Since the pio-

neer settlements of the 1800s, most of the prairie has been plowed and grazed with only a few acres of the original prairie remaining unaltered—fragments of Colorado's rich natural history. A portion of a 15-acre loess prairie is located here. The area was designated a Colorado Natural Area in 1988 by the State of Colorado and the United States Bureau of Reclamation to protect the unique grassland that's part of Colorado's natural heritage. To get to the park and the SWA from Burlington, go 21 miles north on Highway 385 to County Road 2, or a bit north to County Road 3. Turn east on either road to reach the reservoir. *www.parks.state.co.us* and *www.wildlife.state.co.us*

Bonny Lake State Wildlife Area

Elbert County
Elizabeth

One of my favorite rural drives in Eastern Colorado is Highway 86 from Franktown east to I-70 across a rolling prairie landscape sprinkled with intermittent views of the Front Range. Quaint and quintessentially western, the town of Elizabeth is located east of Franktown in the western portion of Elbert County and approximately 45 miles southeast of Denver. With an elevation of 6,530 feet, the town's unique pine-forested setting creates a peaceful ambience. In fact, the National Arbor Day Foundation recognized Elizabeth as a Tree City USA. Check out the playground in **Larmer Park** by heading south from Highway 86 on Tabor Street to Elm

Street. **Bandt Park** also has a nice playground. From 86, go south on Elbert Street to Poplar Street. *www.townofelizabeth.org*

Kiowa

Just east of Elizabeth, Kiowa provides another example of small-town USA with a cowboy feel. Look for **A.F. Nordman Memorial Park** on the south side of Highway 86 at Arapahoe Street.

Simla

Settled in the 1880s, Simla was incorporated in 1913 and served as a shipping center for the area's potato harvest each year. Kids will have fun at the playground at the **Big Sandy School** at 619 Pueblo Avenue.

Larmer Park

Bandt Park

Lincoln County

Limon

Limon is known as the "Hub City" of Eastern Colorado because I-70 and Highways 24, 40, 287, 71, and 86 all cross paths here. Because of its central location for many transportation routes, Limon has become a major gateway to Denver, Colorado Springs, Colorado's mountains, and the Pikes Peak Region. *www.townoflimon.com*

Limon Community Building Playground is on D Avenue between 4th and 5th Streets. Take either Limon Exit from I-70 to Main Street/Highway 24. Go north on D Avenue to the park on the left. **Limon Skate Park** is at C Avenue and 6th Street, not far from the playground, and you can hop on the **Limon Pedestrian Bike Trail** there, too.

Hugo

Hines Park Playground is located at 7th Street and 3rd Avenue in Hugo. From Highway 40/287, head north on 3rd Avenue to the park.

Limon Community Building Playground

Limon Pedestrian Bike Trail

Limon Skate Park

Kit Carson County
For a taste of classic small-town America, check out the tiny agrarian communities that line I-70 between Limon and Burlington. Each one has a pretty little park with a playground—perfect for a midday break while traveling I-70.

Flagler Park and Playground

Seibert Community Park and Playground

Bethune Park and Playground

Flagler
If you're heading east from Limon, Flagler Park and Playground will be your first stop. Take the Flagler Exit north from I-70 to 2nd Avenue. The park is on the left.

Seibert
Seibert lies east of Flagler on I-70. Seibert Community Park and Playground is at 4th Street and Kansas Avenue. Take the Seibert Exit north from I-70 to 4th Street, and head east to the park.

Stratton
Among the rolling wheat and irrigated cornfields of Eastern Colorado lies the community of Stratton. Located 150 miles east of Denver along I-70, Stratton is primarily a farming and ranching community. Stratton Park and the John G. Clark Municipal Pool and Tennis Courts are at 2nd Street and Illinois. Take the Stratton Exit north from I-70 to Highway 24. Go east to Illinois, then north two blocks to the park.

Bethune
The tiny community of Bethune lies just west of Burlington and east of Stratton. Bethune Park and Playground is at 1st Avenue and B Street. Take the Bethune Exit north from I-70, and cross Highway 24. Go right on 1st to the park.

Burlington
The Chicago, Rock Island and Pacific Railroad built a depot at the present site of Burlington, which is located 13 miles from the Colorado-Kansas border. Trains began running in 1888. Burlington Swimming Pool provides a much-needed cooling-off place for the family traveling I-70 in the summer. You'll find it at 480 18th Street. From I-70, take the Highway 385/Burlington Exit north past Highway 24 to Martin Avenue. Go east to the pool at 18th Street.

Kit Carson Recreation Park

Cheyenne County
Kit Carson

Kit Carson Recreation Park is more than 20 years-old, and was recently renovated in a joint venture of the Kit Carson Recreation District and Kit Carson R-1 School District. It's a great place for people of all ages to gather and recreate. The park lies at Church Street and 5th Avenue. Take Church Street north from Highway 40/287 to the park.

Cheyenne Wells

Cheyenne Wells got its name from the Cheyenne American Indians and their water well. Originally located near the fork of the Smokey Hill River, which is five miles north of its present location, the town was a regular stop for the stagecoach line from Kansas City to Denver. Today, the community's main source of income stems from small grain farmers and cattle ranchers. Medicine Arrow Park offers horseshoe pits, playground equipment, restrooms facilities, as well as a lighted half-mile cement walking path, lighted regulation size basketball court, and picnic area. Located at South 2nd Street and West 6th Street just north of Highway 40. *www.townofcheyennewells.com*

Crowley County
Olney Springs

McClure Park is four acres and a place for some rest and play. Take North Gould Avenue north from Highway 96 almost to D Avenue. McClure Park is on the left.

Crowley

Crowley Playground contains mostly basketball courts, so why not have some fun shooting hoops with the kids? It's on Broadway three blocks north of Highway 96.

Ordway

Head north from Highway 96 on Colorado Boulevard to South Park at 5th Street. The generous-size park contains dozens of stately deciduous trees.

Kiowa County
Haswell

Haswell Roadside Park is on the south side of Highway 96. The park has walkways, grills, picnic tables, and play structures.

South Park

Haswell Roadside Park

Eads

Head north on Maine (yes, "Maine"!) Street from Highway 96/287 to lovely **Horseshoe Park** with the big, beautiful trees.

Sheridan Lake

Another small park, **Sheridan Lake Park** is located on the east side of Highway 385/Colorado Avenue as you drive through town.

Pueblo County
Pueblo
Arkansas River Complex

The **Historic Arkansas Riverwalk of Pueblo,** aka HARP, is a 32-acre urban waterfront "experience" that is open to the public daily. The Arkansas River and Pueblo have a long history. For more than 300 years, it was considered the town's lifeblood. Native Americans hunted and trapped along the river, early settlers came as sheepherders and cattlemen, agriculture thrived in Pueblo's warmer climate, and a large manufacturing center depended on the river's vast resources. Interestingly, at various times in history, four nations have claimed ownership of the Arkansas River at HARP's current location: Mexico, Spain, France and the Republic of Texas.

In the 1920s, the Arkansas River was diverted due to a devastating flood that destroyed

much of Pueblo. As the town grew, its riverfront became neglected. Using San Antonio's successful riverwalk as a model, civic leaders planned a restoration that would incorporate shops, cafes, and paths. Pueblo's new riverwalk not only redirected the river to its historic downtown location, but also helped revitalize the area. Attractively designed, HARP serves as a tourist destination and community gathering place, a source of economic stimulus for the town and region, and more. Walk along the riverwalk and you'll see an outdoor amphitheater, lakeside promenade, as well as sculptures, fountains, plazas, indigenous plants, and hand-carved benches. Note the wall design made with original Arkansas River stone. Pedestrian paths in the area link to other pathways, including a trail to Lake Pueblo that passes the Nature & Raptor Center (see below).

The Riverwalk Welcome Center is located at 101 S. Union Avenue. From southbound I-25, take Exit 98B/1st Street, turning right off the ramp. Cross Santa Fe and Main Streets and turn left on Union Avenue. Cross Grand Avenue and the bridge with flags. Park behind the red brick Olde Town Carriage House if you cannot find parking on the street. *www.puebloharp.com*

The **Nature & Raptor Center of Pueblo** (formerly Greenway & Nature Center) is located in beautiful Rock Canyon on the banks of the Arkansas River. A variety of plants and animals live among the center's aquatic, riparian, transition, and semi-arid grassland habitats. The center offers hands-on environmental educational programs, classes, field trips, and other learning opportunities. A spectacular setting for outdoor activities, the center offers bird watching, wildlife viewing, horseback riding, hiking, and boundless opportunities to explore nature in a variety of habitats. On-site amenities include horseshoe pits, volleyball courts, bicycle rentals, and a large playground. One of the most popular attractions is the raptor facility, founded in 1981 and recognized for its rehabilitation efforts. Each year, more than 200 injured and orphaned birds of prey are admitted to the facility from throughout southeastern Colorado with the goal of returning the rehabbed birds to the wild. In fact, half of the raptors are returned while others remain at the center due to permanent disabilities. These resident raptors serve a vital role in the center's educational efforts. Visitors to the raptor facility are able to

Arkansas River Trail

observe some of these feathered patients, which include eagles, hawks, and owls. Open year-round with on-site parking, the center has its own full-service restaurant, so why not make a day of it? Take the Highway 50 West Exit from I-25, and head west to North Pueblo Boulevard. Go south about 2.5 miles to Nature Center Road. Go west for a little more than a mile to the center on your left adjacent to the Arkansas River. *www.natureandraptor.org*

Traveling right past the Nature & Raptor Center, the **Arkansas River Trail** is a paved multi-use path that is popular with both bicyclists and walkers. Following the Arkansas River for 14 miles from Runyon Lake just east of I-25 to the North Marina at Lake Pueblo State Park, the trail offers splendid scenery that includes riparian woodlands and overhanging rock formations. Heading west gets you to the portion of the trail that travels around Lake Pueblo near the popular 150-foot fishing pier. Bring your fishing rod or just take a break to enjoy the view. Heading west is the more popular route for birders and those desiring a more relaxed outing. Heading east on the trail from the Nature & Raptor Center leads you to the Pueblo Whitewater Park downtown. Although not quite as scenic as the other direction, you'll find plenty of dining options along the way. This one trail provides stops along the way at the following locations: Lake Pueblo State Park, the Pueblo Nature Center, Zoo, City Park, the Arkansas River and Fountain Creek, Runyon Lake, the Historic Arkansas Riverwalk of Pueblo (HARP), the Historic Union Avenue area, the downtown area, and the Pueblo Mall. This is an amazing array of opportunities accessible from one bike path! The Fountain Creek, Wildhorse Creek, and Phipps Creek trails combine with the Arkansas River Trail to offer more than 36 miles of river trail in Pueblo.

Although the cities of Colorado Springs and Pueblo are 45 miles apart and lie in separate counties, they are inextricably connected by Fountain Creek. The proposed Colorado Front Range Trail will eventually connect the Arkansas River Trail to the Pikes Peak Greenway (see Colorado Springs, 112). The six-mile section of Fountain Creek Trail that runs through Pueblo already connects to the

Nature & Raptor Center of Pueblo

Arkansas River Trail system and together, these two trails constitute one of the largest sections of completed trails designated by the Colorado Division of Parks and Wildlife as the Front Range Trail in the Southern Colorado region. Once complete, the Front Range Trail project will link together communities along the Front Range from Wyoming to New Mexico. *www.pueblo.us*

The **Pueblo Whitewater Park** is located in downtown Pueblo within walking distance of shops and restaurants in the Historic Downtown District between Union Avenue and the West 4th Street Bridge. The park has eight drops and is approximately 1/2 mile long. The south bank has the world's largest mural. The names of the drops and pools reflect the paintings, Harpo, Marley, and the Grim Reaper, to name a few. Access points to the river and trail are all on the west side of the river. The main access is from Chapa Place south of

West 4th Street. Take out is at Union Avenue. There is a parking lot located on the south side of the Main Street Bridge on the left. You can also park on West Corona Avenue at South Union Avenue. *www.pueblo.us*

Open year-round, the **Pueblo Zoo** is located in City Park. Visitors, including those with strollers or wheelchairs, can enjoy beautifully landscaped grounds that lead to Serengeti Safari, North American Grasslands, the Australian Outback, World of Color, and an Asian Adventure. In the Ecocenter, visitors explore a tropical rain forest, discover naked mole rats in their underground world, and watch penguins "fly" underwater. Islands of Life invites you on a shipwreck journey to habitats around the world. Home to more than 420 animals of 140 species, the zoo is managed by the Pueblo Zoological Society and accredited by the American Zoo and Aquarium Association.

Pueblo Whitewater Park

The North American River Otter Exhibit at the Pueblo Zoo is very popular with visitors who watch the underwater gymnastics of Thelma, Odin, Thorin and Freyja. Swimming up to the glass, the otters playfully interact with visitors, showing off their amazing agility and speed. Formerly among North America's most prevalent mammals, otters have been heavily "harvested" since the European colonization of America for their luxurious fur, and because of erroneous beliefs that they deplete game fish. In many states, including Colorado, they were exterminated. Since 1976, more than 4,000 otters have been successfully reintroduced in 21 states, and these important bio-indicators are once more helping to keep Colorado's aquatic environments healthy. From I-25, take Highway 50 west to Pueblo Boulevard. Go south to Goodnight Avenue. Turn left into City Park and go through the park to the Pueblo Zoo entrance. *www.pueblozoo.org*

Lake Pueblo State Park, considered a fishing hot spot, provides approximately 60 miles of shoreline and an 11-mile-long body of water. Two full-service marinas and a diversity of campsites ensure that guests will stay awhile. Water sports include sailing, motor boating, waterskiing, river tubing, kayaking below the cliff bands, and excellent fishing. Two boat ramps are available. Other outdoor activities include hiking, biking, and picnicking. Hop on one of the many trails and explore the shady shores of the Arkansas River below the dam or the amazing 200-year-old juniper trees. On a clear day, enjoy breathtaking views of the Greenhorn Mountain and the rest of the Wet Mountains to the southwest and the imposing Pikes Peak to the north.

Lake Pueblo's variety of habitats offers diverse wildlife. Along the river corridor, you'll see several beaver dams and lodges, you might spot mule deer, raccoons, and coyotes, and if you're lucky, you could even catch a glimpse of a resident family of bobcats. When visiting the east end of the park, look for soft-shell and snapping turtles residing in the smaller ponds. The shale bluffs throughout the park make ideal habitats for nesting red tail hawks, prairie rattlesnakes, and a rare lizard, the Triploid Checkered Whiptail, of which the entire population is female! Prairie dog towns thrive in the park's shortgrass prairie, and the lake itself is home to a wide variety of waterfowl, from grebes to pelicans. Winter brings great blue herons and gulls, as well as bald eagles, which are celebrated each February during the Eagle Day Festival. Take I-25 to Pueblo, then Highway 50 west. Drive four miles to Pueblo Boulevard, turn south, and go four miles to Thatcher Boulevard/Highway 96. Turn west and go four miles to the south park entrances. Or, take Highway 50 west seven miles to McCulloch Boulevard. Turn south and go four miles to Nichols Road, then turn south and go one mile to the north park entrance. *www.parks.state.co.us*

Pueblo Skateboard Park is located north of City Park's Lake Joy. The park is named after Sergeant Blake A. Harris, who pushed to have the park built in 1999. Sergeant Harris served

Lake Pueblo State Park

in the 1st Cavalry of Fort Hood Texas, and was killed in action in 2007 while serving in Iraq. From I-25, take Highway 50 west to Pueblo Boulevard. Go south to Goodnight Avenue and turn left into City Park. *www.pueblo.us*

Pete Jimenez Park is named after Pete Jimenez, who served with the 29th Infantry Division during World War II, one of the most vicious combats in history. Jimenez was awarded the French Croix de Guerre—"war cross" in English, equivalent of the Medal of Honor—for heroism, valor, bravery, and gallantry in battle. Go south from West 18th Street on Graham Avenue to the park at the dead end.

Runyon Lake State Wildlife Area

Lovell Park

Runyon Lake State Wildlife Area, aka Fountain Lakes, located next to the Arkansas River near the center of Pueblo. Runyon is an excellent place to find birds, particularly in winter when warm water attracts waterfowl and gulls. Mammals in the area include red fox, rabbits, and squirrels. There's also a great paved trail for hiking and biking. Go south on I-25 to Exit 98-A, then south on Santa Fe to the first left, which is Locust Street. Continue for one-half mile past Runyon Field Road to the area. *www.wildlife.state.co.us*

Pueblo West

The 21-acre **Lovell Park** is Pueblo West's largest developed park. Amenities include a covered pavilion picnic area, 25-meter heated outdoor swimming pool, sand volleyball court, paved basketball court, equipped playground for children, as well as three ball fields (two are lighted), horseshoe pits, and public restrooms. From I-25, take Highway 50 west past Pueblo Boulevard to South Purcell Boulevard. Go west on East Hahn's Peak Avenue to the park on your left.

Colorado City

Colorado City offers a nice diversion while driving I-25 south on a hot summer day—especially **Greenhorn Meadows Park.** Have a picnic or get some exercise on Greenhorn's ball fields and playground. The park also has a campground. Check out Greenhorn Valley Arts and Music Festival, held at the park each July. From I-25, take the Colorado City Exit south of Pueblo onto Highway 165. The park is three miles on your left. *www.cocityparksandrec.com*

Greenhorn Meadows Park

Otero County
Manzanola

East of Rocky Ford on Highway 50 is the little town of Manzanola and its cute **Train Depot Park** located at Park and South Railroad streets. Go north on Park Street from Highway 50.

Rocky Ford

The tiny agricultural town of Rocky Ford and its surrounding Arkansas River Valley are

Babcock Park

considered Colorado's melon-producing capital. In late summer, roadside stands open for business, and cantaloupe and watermelons are shipped and sold nationwide. The annual Arkansas Valley Fair is held in Rocky Ford every August. Join the locals to celebrate the area's diverse cultures and outstanding agricultural community with a variety of events including a rodeo, carnival, crafts, food, and much more. On Watermelon Day during the fair, watermelons are free for the taking. History attributes much of Rocky Ford's agricultural successes to George W. Swink, who settled in the area in 1871 from Illinois, developed the watermelon and cantaloupe industry, and helped create the canal system known as Rocky Ford Ditch. According to the Rocky Ford History Museum, after crossing a ford with a shale and rock bottom, the legendary Kit Carson named the town "The Rocky Ford Crossing Place." Visit the museum, located in Library Park, to learn more about Rocky Ford's important place in Colorado's history. While in the area, stop for a picnic at **Babcock Park.** Drive south on Main Street from Highway 50 past Washington Avenue to the park.

La Junta

Located in southeastern Colorado, about 60 miles east of Pueblo, La Junta is the county seat of Otero County. For more than 100 years, La Junta—"the junction" or "the meeting place" in English—has served as a junction for commercial, agricultural, and ranching ventures. Earlier, La Junta was the junction where the

City Park

Sk8Way Skate Park

Santa Fe Trail, one of the country's first great trade routes, branched south to New Mexico, while a lesser route continued west through Pueblo. Although La Junta is situated on the south bank of the Arkansas River amid rolling shortgrass prairieland, the mountains to the west are a familiar sight. Farming dominates the landscape in a narrow corridor along the river, while expansive stretches of grasslands can be found north and south of Highway 50.

La Junta's largest park, **City Park,** offers a playground and lots of shade trees for picnicking on hot summer days. There's plenty of open space and several pavilions for family events. The **Sk8Way Skate Park** is located in the park at 12th Street and Colorado Avenue. Go south on Colorado from Highway 50 to the park on the right. *www.ci.la-junta.co.us*

Cheraw

The new **Cheraw School Community Playground** is located north of Highway 109/Grand Avenue on North 1st Street.

Las Animas City Park

Bent County

Las Animas

Las Animas City Park features an outdoor pool with benches, a bath house, a covered family seating area, and a water slide. Other amenities included a playground, gazebo, volleyball and skateboard areas, as well as horseshoe pits and barbeque grills. The park is located at 6th Street and Park Avenue. Go north on Beech Avenue from Highway 50 to the park on the left. *www.bentcounty.org*

Called "a sapphire on the plains" by some, **John Martin Reservoir State Park** is a year-round paradise for outdoor enthusiasts, nature lovers, and wildlife. You can boat, water-ski, hike, bike, view wildlife, camp, and fish here, with anglers catching walleye, saugeye, bass, wiper, crappie, perch, and catfish. Because nearly 400 bird species have been documented in Bent County, John Martin is a birdwatcher's heaven. Majestic bald eagles roost here in winter, and threatened and endangered species such as the piping plover and the least tern reside in the park for several months each year. Located on a high desert prairie, the area abounds with high rocky bluffs, shortgrass prairie, and flora and fauna. The park's most recognized plant is the yucca or soap-weed plant, which is known for its many medicinal uses dating back to the area's Native American tribes. Sagebrush, prickly pear cactus, buffalo grass, and many tree species also grow here. Take Highway 50 east from La Junta for approximately 20 miles to Las Animas. Proceed east through Las Animas to Hasty, approximately 16 miles. Turn south on School Street and go about two miles. The visitor center is on the right as the road curves to the east. *www.parks.state.co.us*

Prowers County
Lamar

The Lamar Swimming Pool complex can help beat the heat of summer. It's located at 1107 Parkview Avenue, the same place as Lamar's beautiful Willow Creek Park. From Highway 385/287/Main Street on the south end of town, head east on Memorial Drive to the park.

Holly

Holly Gateway Park is located at the site of "Old Horse Creek," which once ran through town from north to south, but was diverted several years ago. The original creek bed was planted with trees and grass, and now offers a nice green area in the middle of town. The site of the annual Blue Grass Festival each June, Gateway Park contains playground equipment, park tables, and a shelter awning with a concrete floor. Driving through town, you'll find it on the north side of Highway 50. *www.townofholly.com*

Las Animas County
Trinidad

Historic Kit Carson Park provides bike paths, ball fields, and a Victorian bandshell and playground. The park also is the site of a huge cast bronze sculpture of Kit Carson, considered one of the finest equestrian statues in the country. It's located at 930 San Pedro Street at Kansas Avenue. Take North Commercial Street north under I-25 to East Kansas

Avenue, then turn right into the park. The enormous Trinidad Skate Park features lots of lines, no kinks, and fast full-arena runs. Rated ninth in the world by champion skater Tony Hawk, kids—and a few adults—love to "carve it up" here. Check it out by taking Exit 13 off I-25 to Main Street. Then turn right at Santa Fe Trail, left at Jefferson Street, and right at the bottom of the hill on Beshoar. You'll find Trinidad's Family Aquatic Center in the same location.

For a town of its size, Trinidad's public green spaces are second to none. Central Park and Playground is worth the trip. Take North Animas Street west under I-25 to Prospect-Street, then south to the park on Stonewall Avenue.

Central Park and Playground

Heart of Trinidad River Trail

Heart of Trinidad River Trail runs along the Purgatoire River from Carbon Street to Chestnut Street, and Commercial Street to Linden Street. Eventually, the Purgatoire River Trail will run along the river all the way to Trinidad Lake State Park. *www.treasuretrinidad.com*

Just a few minutes west of Trinidad on Highway 12, **Trinidad Lake State Park** provides an ideal setting for water sports. The park's hefty lake combined with the region's mild climate make it an enticing draw for anglers, who catch rainbow and brown trout, largemouth bass, channel catfish, walleye, crappie and bluegill. Boaters of all types enjoy the open waters and modern services, and miles of trails provide spectacular scenery and abundant opportunities for hiking, biking, or exploring

Trinidad Lake State Park

nature. The Long's Canyon Trail provides one of the best examples of the geologic K-T Boundary anywhere in the country, and is a serious attraction and work of study for geologists.

The park has a vast array of plants: Pinyon-juniper woodlands occur on rocky outcrops and slopes over one-third of the park, with shortgrass and mixed-grass prairies also occupying park uplands. The park's overstory is dominated by pinyon pine, one-seed juniper, and Rocky Mountain juniper, while scrubland species such as Gambel oak, mountain mahogany, and serviceberry reside in the understory. The forests are home to a variety of wildlife such as the pinion jay, roadrunners, and a host of other bird species, as well as deer, elk, and various smaller animals. Heading south on I-25, take Exit 14. At the stoplight, continue straight ahead to the next stop sign. Follow directions to Highway 12 and head west for three miles to the park. *www.parks.state.co.us*

Further west on Highway 12, **Bosque del Oso State Wildlife Area** is the largest state wildlife area in Colorado at 30,000 acres. Bosque del Oso contains critical habitat for elk, black bear, turkey, deer, and bald and golden eagles. Note that the area is closed from December through April to protect bald eagles and wintering elk. This huge SWA is comprised of pinyon-juniper woodlands with some mixed-conifer on the north-facing slopes, abundant shrubland and oak habitats, as well as a few riparian groves along the Purgatoire River. Two streams flow through the refuge: the middle fork and south fork of the Purgatoire River, both providing catch-and-release fishing with flies and lures. Hunting is by limited license for deer, elk, black bear, and turkey. From Trinidad, take Exit 14A off I-25, and go west on Highway 12 approximately 21 miles to the town of Weston. Look for access signs between Weston and the next town, Stonewall. The property is south of the highway. Be aware this area is heavily impacted by a coalbed methane gas extraction infrastructure. You will see energy service vehicles operating on roads between 9:00 a.m. and 3:00 p.m. *www.wildlife. state.co.us* and *www.historictrinidad.com*

Bosque del Oso State Wildlife Area

Kim Equine Pavilion

Aguilar

The historic town of Aguilar has a Town Park on the east side of Main Street. Take the Aguilar I-25 Business Exit to reach Main Street.

Kim

Kim may be small in size but it has a huge spirit fostered by the hard-working ranch families of Las Animas County. This spirit is evident in the Community Playground located downtown and in the Kim Equine Pavilion horse arena and rodeo grounds located at the north end of town on Highway 160.

Kim Community Playground

Baca County
Springfield

Springfield's hot summers bring temperatures to 90 degrees or more. Cool off in the Springfield Pool located at 401 East 7th Avenue. Prairie Park Playground is located in Springfield City Park at 5th Avenue and Tipton Street. From Highway 385/287, head west on 5th Avenue/Longhorn Drive to the park. *www.springfieldcolorado.com*

Walsh

East of Springfield in Walsh, look for the lovely Walsh City Park at Maplewood and North Colorado Streets. Go south from Highway 160 on North Illinois Street to the park. Walsh has a Community Pool at 500 East Oak Street—a good thing since Walsh gets just as hot as Springfield in the summer!

Northwest Colorado

Northwest Colorado

Larimer County
Fort Collins

The giant 17,500-square-foot **Edora Skate Park** features snake runs, bowls, ramps, and rails for various skill levels. The park is free and open to the public year-round with an integrated design that allows for a seamless flow between structures. It's located just southwest of Timberline and Prospect Roads at 1420 East Stuart Street, between the Edora Pool Ice Center and the ball fields at **Edora Park.** Get there by taking the city's transit system or via Spring Creek Trail. Go to *www.fcgov.com* for information about Fort Collins' remarkable inventory of recreation opportunities, parks, trails, and open space.

Situated on 100 acres nestled against the Fort Collins foothills, **Spring Canyon Community Park** features a two-acre dog park complete with a lake for our furry pals who love to swim, a free ride mountain biking course, and **Inspiration Playground,** Colorado's first universally-accessible playground. An outdoor space for children and families of all abilities to share activities and recreation, Inspiration Playground enables children with and without disabilities to play independently on the same equipment. The play surface allows for wheel-chairs, walkers, and support braces, and the safe, state-of-the-art, sensory-rich structures encourage integration and the development of cognitive, emotional, physical and social skills.

Spring Canyon Community Park also features traditional amenities such as picnic shelters, trails, open turf areas, ball fields, lighted basketball and tennis courts, Art in Public Places projects, and scenic landscapes. The park is adjacent to Cottonwood Glen Neighborhood Park and Pine Ridge Natural Area, and it connects to the Spring Creek and Fossil Creek Trails, both segments of Fort Collins' trail system. Spring Canyon Community Park and Inspiration Playground are located at 2626 West Horsetooth in southwest Fort Collins at the west terminus of Horsetooth Road. Parking lots are located at either end of the park—on the north side at Overland Trail and on the south side at Horsetooth Road. *www.fcgov.com/parks*

Cathy Fromme Prairie is a rare example of Fort Collins' pre-settlement shortgrass prairie landscape. Eagles and hawks frequent the area's many prairie dog colonies, and horned lizards, ground-nesting songbirds, butterflies, rabbits, coyotes, and rattlesnakes also reside here. Visit the raptor observatory built into the hillside

Inspiration Playground

(near the Shields Street entrance) to view the hawks and eagles, especially during the cold weather months. The paved **Fossil Creek Trail** runs through the prairie for 2.5 miles. A variety of trails run along Fossil Creek stretching through Fort Collins' southern region, including those at Fossil Creek Park, and the sizeable wetlands and natural area around Fossil Creek Reservoir, which can be accessed from Carpenter Road just west of I-25 (at Fossil Creek Reservoir Regional Open Space). You'll find Cathy Fromme Prairie southwest of Shields Street and Harmony Road in southwest Fort Collins. *www.fcgov.com*

The peaceful and serene **Fossil Creek Reservoir Regional Open Space Park** features wetlands, rolling prairie uplands, and a tree-lined reservoir. Designated an Important Bird Area by the National Audubon Society, this natural area supplies crucial habitat to bald eagles (in winter), raptors and a variety of shorebirds, songbirds, and waterfowl species. Coyotes, deer, and prairie dogs also make their homes here. Don't forget to bring your camera, binoculars, or spotting scope—there's much to see! Artists might also want to bring along their sketchbooks.

Cathy Fromme Prairie and Fossil Creek Trail

Horsetooth Reservoir

Fossil Creek Reservoir Regional Open Space was created through a partnership between the City of Fort Collins, Larimer County, and North Poudre Irrigation Company to conserve 843 acres. Fort Collins' Natural Areas Department manages the site, including restoration and stewardship, trail and site maintenance, snow removal, volunteer opportunities, and education programs. Conservation of natural resources while providing public recreation is the highest priority. Trails have been designed to minimize human impact on sensitive wildlife; biking, boating, fishing, and pets are not permitted here. Open daily from dawn to dusk, Fossil Creek is located on Carpenter Road/County Road 32, approximately one mile west of I-25, or two miles east of Timberline on the north side of Carpenter Road. *www.fcgov.com/naturalareas*

Horsetooth Reservoir features abundant protected open space and recreational opportunities. Jointly operated by the Bureau of Reclamation and the Northern Colorado Water Conservancy District, the reservoir is part of the Colorado-Big Thompson Project to divert water from the west slope to the east slope for drinking water, irrigation, and hydropower generation. Larimer County manages recreation at the 6.5-mile reservoir, which gets plenty of use. Along with 1,900 acres of surrounding public lands, the reservoir provides opportunities for fishing, boating, camping,

Fossil Creek Reservoir Regional Open Space Park

picnicking, swimming, scuba diving, rock climbing, and water skiing. From I-25 north, take the Harmony Road/Timnath Exit. Go west on Harmony Road/County Road 38E for about 11 miles to the entrance at the reservoir's south end. *http://larimer.org/parks*

Horsetooth Mountain Open Space actually comprises three different open spaces—Culver, Soderberg, and Hughey. A picturesque 2,711 acres, Horsetooth's elevations range from 5,430 to 7,255 feet. The park offers 29 miles of hiking, biking, and horseback riding trails, which connect to the Blue Sky and Lory State Park Trails. A massive rock formation on top of the mountain, Horsetooth Rock makes for a highly-visible landmark from the plains. Horsetooth Falls, with its cascading waterfalls in late spring and impressive views of the Front Range, add to the allure. Follow the directions above to the Horsetooth Reservoir South Bay entrance, then continue west on County Road 38E about 2.5 miles from the South Bay Entrance or one mile from the Inlet

Bay Entrance (Shoreline Drive). Look for the parking area and trailhead on the north side of the road. *http://larimer.org/parks*

From rolling valleys to mountainous hillsides, **Lory State Park's** 26 miles of trails rarely exceed a 12 percent grade. The variety of trails allows for short-to-long distance hiking, jogging, mountain biking, and horseback riding. Folks looking for more of a remote getaway can choose the backcountry camping option. Trails on Lory's east side offer access to some of Horsetooth Reservoir's bays and coves. Canoeists, kayakers, and rafters can hand-launch their crafts within a short walk from the North Eltuck Bay parking lot, and power boaters can launch at the Horsetooth Dam nearby Horsetooth Reservoir. Take Harmony Road/County Road 38E west from I-25. As you approach the reservoir, turn north onto County Road 23N to the T-intersection. Turn left onto County Road 42C and head north to Lodgepole Drive. Turn left and go 1.6 miles to the park entrance. *www.parks.state.co.us*

Horsetooth Mountain Open Space

Lory State Park

Loveland

Situated at the western-most edge of the plains with spectacular views of Long's Peak, **Boyd Lake State Park** offers activities for visitors of all ages. A haven for water lovers in particular, the 1,700-surface-acre lake sees plenty of action including fishing, swimming, and a wide range of boating. Boyd Lake's sandy beach and pavilion are popular spots in the summer. With 148 paved pull-through sites, camping is also popular here, as well as picnicking, hiking, biking, hunting, and wildlife and bird watching. More than 200 species of migratory and resident birds have been observed in this area, including great blue herons, egrets, great-horned owls, hawks, eagles, and white pelicans. Wildlife moves in and out with the seasons. It's common to spot white pelicans in the summer; in the winter, bald eagles are often seen perching on ice next to open water. Coyotes, raccoons, muskrats, cottontail rabbits, red foxes, and ground squirrels are also often seen. Anglers come to catch rainbow trout, walleye, largemouth and white bass, yellow perch, crappie, channel catfish, and carp. From I-25, take Exit 257, and travel west on Highway 34/East Eisenhower Boulevard to Madison Avenue. Go north to East 37th Street, turn east, and go about one-half mile to where it curves north and is renamed County Road 11-C. Boyd Lake State Park is on the east side of this road. *www.parks.state.co.us*

An historic working horse and cattle ranch, **Sylvan Dale Guest Ranch** offers a wide range of services, from bed-and-breakfast retreats to ranch vacations, complete with optional cattle drives and rounds-ups. The 3,200-acre dude ranch located near Rocky Mountain National Park nudges the banks of the Big Thompson River. It's against this beautiful backdrop that guests go on trail rides and overnight pack trips, take horseback riding lessons, and play "gymkhana"—games on horseback. Guests can fly fish for trophy trout, play tennis, swim, and enjoy numerous other activities. You're sure to encounter the ranch's famous cattle while staying here, whether you're rounding them up or watching them graze. (The grass-fed, locally-raised and processed Heart-J Beef

Boyd Lake State Park

Sylvan Dale Guest Ranch

is delicious and available for purchase.) Owned by the Jessup family since 1946, Sylvan Dale Ranch is committed to preserving the land and wildlife habitat for future generations. During a meeting in 1995 that included four generations, the family developed a master plan to preserve 90 percent of the 3,200 acres via conservation easements—to date, 1,700 acres have been protected. To find the ranch, travel seven miles west of Wilson Boulevard in Loveland on Highway 34. Look for the wooden Sylvan Dale sign between mile markers 84 and 83 before you enter the Big Thompson Canyon. *www.sylvandale.com*

Morey Wildlife Reserve is located near the Big Thompson River, just west of Mariana Butte Golf Course. Managed by Loveland's Parks and Recreation Department, this 27-acre reserve offers exceptional passive recreation

Morey Wildlife Reserve

opportunities such as wildlife viewing, nature study, and environmental education. Access the eight-acre pond by taking a soft-surface trail to its north end and back. The east side of the pond—a wildlife conservation area—isn't open to the public. To protect sensitive natural resources, dogs and other domestic animals are prohibited on the reserve, as are hunting, fishing, jogging, and bicycling. A terrific place for solitude, the reserve is open for walk-in access from sunrise to sunset. Drive west on Highway 34 through Loveland to Rossum Drive. Turn south and proceed to Cedar Valley Drive. Go west to Deer Meadow Court. You can park on Cedar Valley Drive and walk down Deer Meadow Court to the park. *www.ci.loveland.co.us*

Estes Park

The 1,362-acre **Hermit Park Open Space** is a breathtaking property nestled into the hills at elevations ranging from 7,880 to 8,964 feet. Featuring ponderosa pine forests and wetland meadows, the open space offers abundant habitat for a variety of wildlife. Features include a group campground, a pavilion that can be reserved, cabins, RV and tent camping, and a variety of trails for hiking, horseback riding, and mountain biking. *www.co.larimer.co.us*

Hermit Park Open Space

Laramie Foothills
Mountains to Plains Project

Red Mountain Open Space is an important piece of the Mountains to Plains Project, a collaborative land protection effort between many partners that has resulted in the preservation of more than 55,000 acres of this magnificent land. Resource experts developed the Red Mountain Open Space management plan in collaboration with a plan for the adjacent Soapstone Prairie Natural Area (see below).

Located just 25 miles north of Fort Collins, Red Mountain Open Space's roughly 15,000 acres features deep crimson and tan

rocks, rolling grasslands, and sandy washes. This rugged and remote open space boasts exceptional biodiversity, including rare intact plant communities. Due to its significant natural, cultural, agricultural, and recreation values, it's an ideal area for conservation—and a great place for watching wildlife, with species from both plains and mountains residing here. Red Mountain Open Space also has a rich history of human culture, dating back to a time before the Egyptian pyramids were built. History has it that some of North America's first humans lived in this area more than 12,000 years ago, and people have lived on and worked the land ever since. Out of respect for these cultures, collecting artifacts is prohibited. You'll find the Red Mountain Open Space trailhead on County Road 23, about an hour north of Fort Collins. From here, hikers, bikers, and horseback riders enjoy more than 15 miles of multi-use trails. The Bent Rock Trail is a hiking-only loop. Note: If you find the open space parking lot full, the area is at capacity. Parking is not allowed along the roadway or outside of designated trailhead parking spaces. Head over to Soapstone Prairie Natural Area and come back to Red Mountain Open Space another time! The route to Red Mountain is somewhat circuitous, so make sure to take along a map. From I-25, take Exit 288 west onto County Road 82, and travel about 18 miles north of Fort Collins. From Highway 287 to the west, go one mile north of Livermore, and turn north on County Road 80. The maps at *www.larimer.org/naturalresources* will get you there.

Contiguous with Red Mountain Open Space to the east, **Soapstone Prairie Natural Area** is another extraordinary natural area featuring 18,000 acres of wide-open vistas, nearly pristine grasslands, world-renowned cultural resources, and miles of trails.

Soapstone Prairie contains an extensive and diverse human history that includes Paleoindians of the Ice Age, millenia of American Indian tribes, and more than a century of

Red Mountain Open Space

homesteaders and cattle and sheep ranchers. A National Historic Landmark, the Lindenmeier archeological site is the most well-known cultural site at Soapstone. Excavations in the 1930s dated human habitation to at least 10,000 years ago. Needles, beads, and stone tools were uncovered, making Lindenmeier the most extensive Folsom (Paleoindian) culture site found to date. Other items of historical significance at Soapstone include possible Clovis (pre-Paleoindian) cultural sites, numerous stone rings, sheepherder's stone cairns, as well as ruins of historic homesteads, ranches, their associated buildings, and a schoolhouse foundation.

Visitors at Soapstone Prairie are asked to respect the cultural heritage by staying on designated trails. If you see an artifact—which is highly unlikely—leave it alone as artifacts are important parts of the legacy of those who came before us. Soapstone Prairie is best reached from the east. Follow the directions to Red Mountain from I-25; however, the route will eventually lead you north on County Road 15. See detailed information and directions at *www.fcgov.com/naturalareas*.

The **Cherokee State Wildlife Area** is comprised of five units—the Upper, Middle, Lower, Lone Pine, and Rabbit Creek—encompassing more than 25,000 acres. Home to mule deer, elk, coyotes, a variety of birds, as well as black bear, mountain lion, and moose, Cherokee provides many opportunities for wildlife watching and hunting. Besides deer and elk, in-season hunting of squirrel, dusky grouse, rabbit, and dove is permitted. Camping, trail hiking, and fishing the cold water streams running through the area are other popular activities. Horseback riding and biking are permitted, but only on designated roads and trails. Restrooms are on site. From Fort Collins, drive north on Highway 287, 14 miles north of Ted's Place to West County Road 80C/Cherokee Park Road. Turn left and head west 5.6 miles to the Cherokee State Wildlife Area Lower Unit trailhead and parking lot on the left side of the road. *www.wildlife.state.co.us*

Cherokee State Wildlife Area

Soapstone Prairie Natural Area

Jackson County

Colorado doesn't get much more rugged than **Colorado State Forest State Park.** Stretching along the west side of the Medicine Bow Mountains and into the north end of the Never Summer Range, the park offers 71,000 acres of forest, jagged peaks, alpine lakes, wildlife, seemingly endless miles of trails—and an extremely healthy moose population. If you've never seen a moose, but you'd like to, this is the place to visit. With more than 600 observed year-round, the North Park region is considered the moose-viewing capital of Colorado. The habitat and diversity at State Forest State Park ensures an activity for every season. Favorites include camping, hiking, four-wheeling, horseback riding, skiing, snowshoeing, telemarking, snowboarding, snowmobiling, fishing, hunting, birding, wildlife viewing, and geocaching. If you're the adventurous type, check out one of the seven yurts and two huts, operated by Never Summer Nordic. A backcountry experience can't be beat, and these secure, secluded shelters are comfier than a tent. Be sure to stop by the Moose Visitor Center near Gould on Highway 14. If you'd like to try your hand at geocaching, GPS units are available for rent. From Fort Collins, travel west on Highway 14 for 75 miles across Cameron Pass. *www.parks.state.co.us*

Colorado State Forest State Park

Grand County
Fraser

Connecting the towns of Fraser and Winter Park, the **Fraser River Trail** runs through the valley floor and all the way up to the Winter Park Ski Area. In places, it lies right next to the river. My favorite stretch is unpaved, connecting Cozens Ranch Open Space with downtown Fraser on the east side of Highway 40. The paved portion exists both east and west of the highway on its way through Winter Park, with options for many points of access.

For two miles, the trail bisects the **Cozens Ranch Open Space,** offering biking, hiking, wildlife viewing, several fishing ponds, and

other amenities. Billy Cozens settled the Fraser Valley in the late 1800s; his ranch house is operated today as Cozens Ranch Museum. You can access Cozens Ranch Open Space from the Fraser River Trail where it intersects County Road 804 (by Safeway) or Rendezvous Road (near Millennium Bank). There's a great map of the trail at *www.frasercolorado.com.*

The **Fraser Valley Sports Complex** is a 40-acre park located just outside Fraser on the west side of Highway 40 at County Road 5. The complex is home to an NHL-sized, partially enclosed ice rink known as "The Ice Box," three softball/baseball diamonds, two regulation soccer fields, basketball courts, picnic tables, grills, a sand volleyball court, and a 20-foot by 30-foot picnic shelter. All are available for public use or private rental. *www.fraservalleyrec.org*

Fraser River Trail

One of two YMCA of the Rockies facilities in the Colorado Rocky Mountains, **Snow Mountain Ranch** is located near Winter Park, Rocky Mountain National Park, and Grand Lake. Snow Mountain Ranch provides a gathering place for friends, families, and groups who love outdoor activities complemented by a tranquil setting and incredible scenery. There's certainly no lack of recreational opportunities on the ranch's 5,000 acres. On-site summer activities include horseback riding, hiking, biking, canoeing, a zip line, and a variety of family programs, plus easy access to nearby fishing, boating, and rafting. On-site winter activities include cross-country skiing on one of the most expansive trail systems in the U.S., sledding, snowshoeing, winter family programs, and easy access to the Winter Park, Mary Jane, and Sol Vista downhill ski areas. Affordable accommodations at the ranch include lodge rooms, family cabins, reunion cabins with fireplaces, tent and RV campgrounds, and yurts.

Although the YMCA will continue to own the land, nearly 2,800 acres of Snow Mountain Ranch are protected in perpetuity thanks to a conservation easement. Snow Mountain Ranch is located on County Road 53 west of Highway 40, half-way between the towns of Granby and Fraser. *www.ymcarockies.org*

Winter Park

An ideal place for a family outing, **Hideaway Park** has been completely renovated with a new skate park, picnic pavilion, restroom

Snow Mountain Ranch

facilities, and shade structures. More fun awaits in winter at the park's sledding hill where guests are provided with free sleds. Summer at the park is filled with activities. Bring your picnic dinner on Thursday evenings for free live music, or take advantage of free movie nights. A variety of other entertaining events occur at various times of the year. Be sure to stop by the visitor's center for a list of what's happening while you're in town. Located on the east side of Highway 40 across from the visitor's center in downtown Winter Park. *www.winterparkgov.com*

As you drive up Highway 40 on the way to Winter Park from Denver, stop at the top of the pass and check out the portion of the Continental Divide National Scenic Trail that begins at the **Berthoud Pass Trailhead.** Crossing the highway, the trail runs east into the James Peak Wilderness and west into the Vasquez Peak Wilderness. I've hiked and photographed the entire 750-mile Colorado portion of the trail. If you enjoy alpine scenery, it doesn't get any better than this! Day hikes in either direction from Berthoud Pass are incredibly scenic.

The vision of the **Continental Divide National Scenic Trail,** aka the "King of Trails," is to create

Town Square Park

a 3,100-mile primitive and challenging backcountry trail running from Canada to Mexico. Thousands of volunteers have dedicated nearly $7 million in labor, and individuals, foundations, and businesses have committed many more millions toward the efforts. As of 2011, 2,268 miles of the trail were completed. Maps can be found at a variety of sites including *www.trailsource.com*.

Grand Lake

Town Square Park contains open space, picnic tables, and a fine playground, all with views of spectacular Rocky Mountain National Park. You can't miss it on the north side of Grand Avenue at Garfield Street in the middle of town. *www.townofgrandlake.com*

Hot Sulphur Springs

Pioneer Park lies on the banks of the Colorado River on the east side of town. You'll find campsites with picnic tables and fire rings on the southwest end of the park, between the river and the train tracks near the hot springs. The area also has three day-sites for anglers and other visitors, as well as a group site where several people can camp together. Drive one block north of Highway 40/Byers Avenue to Grand Street. Go west across the river to County Road 20, and watch for the park on the left.

Kremmling

West Grand Community Park has a nice playground and mountain views in all directions. It's on 12th Street south of Highway 40 on the west end of town. **West Grand Community Skate Park** is also on 12th, but north of the highway on the east side of the high school parking lot.

Routt County

The **Yampa River Legacy Project** is an effort to protect the ecological health of the Yampa River and its surrounding agricultural lands, while also providing suitable recreational opportunities. Partners include Steamboat Springs, Craig, and Hayden; Routt and Moffat counties; the Forest Service and Bureau of Land Management; Colorado Parks and Wildlife; the Yampa Valley Land Trust; and The Nature Conservancy. The following are just some of the investments made in this remarkable part of northwest Colorado.

Steamboat Springs

Steamboat Springs offers three major trail systems in and around the city. To the south of town, Emerald Mountain serves as the backdrop for and site of the **Emerald Mountain Trail System.** This city-owned land offers more than 20 miles of multi-use recreational trails for the public. These trails, which pro-

Yampa River Core Trail

Yampa River Legacy Project, Lafarge Pond

vide stunning views of the Yampa River Valley, have been planned and constructed for the public to enjoy and allow for two-way pedestrian, bicycle, and equestrian traffic.

To the north of town, the 5.2-mile, multi-use **Spring Creek Trail** is popular for hiking and biking. Parking is located at the intersection of East Maple Street and Amethyst Street.

The **Yampa River Core Trail,** a seven-mile, multi-use trail, follows the meandering Yampa River from Walton Creek Road and Highway 40 west to the James Brown Bridge on Shield Drive. Cottonwood groves, great fishing, scenic overlook benches, and lovely picnic spots make this trail a great option for a leisurely stroll or commuting through town.

Aspiring ski jumpers will take special interest in the **Howelsen Hill Ski Area.** Holding a unique place in the history of skiing, Howelsen has seen more of its skiers head to international competition than any other ski area in North America. More than 79 Olympians making over 130 Winter Olympic appearances, 15 members of the Colorado Ski Hall of Fame, and six members of the National Ski Hall of fame have made Howelsen their training ground. This famous ski area is also the oldest in continuous use in Colorado, boasting the largest and most complete natural ski jumping complex in North America. Can't stand cold weather? Howelsen offers a brand new summer jumping facility.

Chuck Lewis State Wildlife Area

Howelsen Hill Ski Area

You can get across the Yampa River on 13th or 5th Streets in downtown Steamboat. *www.steamboatsprings.net*

Just east of Steamboat along the Yampa River, **Chuck Lewis State Wildlife Area** features extraordinary scenery including hay meadows, wetlands, and gorgeous views up and down the Yampa. Photograph the hay bales at summer's end with the ski area in the background, or catch a shot of elk congregating along the river in the winter. Drive south from Steamboat on Highway 40, and make a right on Highway 131. Where the highway curves 90 degrees to the east, go straight on county road 14F. There are great photos to be made where the road crosses the Yampa River. *www.wildlife.state.co.us*

Steamboat Lake State Park and **Pearl Lake State Park** lie 25 and 23 miles respectively, north of Steamboat in the Elk River Valley. One of the most beautiful ranching valleys in the West, let alone in Colorado, the Elk River

Steamboat Lake State Park

Valley contains dozens of working cattle ranches, most of which have been permanently protected from development by conservation easements. To the west, you'll find views of the Elkhead Mountains and to the east, the Park Range of the Mount Zirkel Wilderness. I've taught a number of photography workshops in the valley over the years; it's one of my favorite places in Colorado to photograph, offering exceptional pictures in all four seasons.

Slightly east of the Elk River Road, Pearl Lake State Park is nestled in the mountains in a quiet forest setting. Surrounded by mountains and trees, campers pitch their tents and park their trailers along the lake and up a gentle hill. Anglers revel in the excellent fly and lure

fishing of native cutthroat trout, which are easily recognizable by their bright red throats. Hikers can follow the shoreline trail deep into the forest, and picnickers love the picture-perfect ambience of the big trees framing the lake—a perfect spot for reflection photos. Pearl Lake is indeed a nature-lover's escape.

Hahn's Peak frames the breathtaking scenery of Steamboat Lake State Park. There's plenty to do here, and in such a beautiful setting: family fishing, camping, picnicking, trails for hiking and exploring, swimming at the swim beach, and boating with the amenity of a full-service marina. The hay meadows surrounded by aspen forests are incredibly photogenic each season, but it's the reflections of the Mount Zirkel Wilderness in Steamboat

Carpenter Ranch

Lake that draw me back year after year! County Road 62 circumvents the west side of the park from the little town of Clark, home of a popular general store that's open year-round—and the place to stock up while visiting the park.

Routt National Forest helps to preserve large tracts of contiguous habitat in the region, which a variety of wildlife calls home. Mule deer and red fox are commonly seen, and rare sightings of black bears and mountain lions are sometimes reported. American martens, long-tailed weasels, northern pocket gophers, beavers, muskrats, and several species of shrews, voles, squirrels, and mice are also often spotted at Steamboat Lake, as well as tiger salamanders, striped chorus frogs, and western

terrestrial garter snakes. Because Steamboat Lake doesn't experience drastic late summer drawdowns, the reservoir's shoreline conditions and water levels remain more constant for resident and migrating wildlife.

Steamboat Lake State Park is also home to more than 200 species of migratory and resident birds, including the northern harrier, osprey, great blue heron, western screech owl, western bluebird, hairy and downy woodpeckers, and red-winged blackbird. Located in the Pacific Flyway, the reservoir attracts many shorebirds and waterfowl. Greater sandhill cranes return to nest in the willow carrs and marshes each spring. Park officials ask visitors to keep their distance when observing this special bird species. Steamboat offers excellent cold-water fishing for rainbow trout, Tasmanian and bel-aire hybrids, cutthroat and brown trout, with an occasional brook trout reported.

The spectacular snow-covered valley and mountains provide plenty of winter fun for outdoor lovers. Snowmobiling, ice fishing, and serene cross-country skiing and snowshoeing are a few of the cold weather sports to enjoy here. Try out one of the park's 10 cozy camper cabins down by the marina—some featuring a wonderful winter's view of the lake or mountains. Drive west through downtown Steamboat until you get to the stoplight at Elk River Road/County Road 129. Go right and you're on your way into the Elk River Valley. *www.parks.state.co.us*

Hayden

Carpenter Ranch was acquired by The Nature Conservancy in 1996 as the centerpiece of its broader effort to conserve the natural and agricultural heritage of the Yampa River Valley. Today, it's a working cattle ranch, a research and education facility, and a center for cooperation and dialogue. A walk through the rare cottonwood riparian forest offers opportunities to view 150 species of birds that nest or migrate through here. The education facility features interactive exhibits, historical background, and information about the many species that live here. The Yampa River supports one of the world's largest remaining examples of a rare riparian forest dominated by narrowleaf cottonwood, box elder, and red-osier dogwood.

Open to the public from May 15 to September 1, Thursday through Saturday, 9 a.m. to noon, the ranch is approximately 20 miles west of Steamboat Springs on the north side of Highway 40. Look for a white Carpenter Ranch sign on the north side of the road, and then turn down the dirt road and park at the visitor center. *www.nature.org*

Yampa River State Park is located in the beautiful Yampa Valley west of Steamboat Springs. A variety of cottonwood trees are ubiquitous along the Yampa River—the lime greens in May, and yellow and orange leaves in September and October provide massive color for the landscape photographer! Yampa River State Park is actually three parks in one: the park headquarters located about three miles west of Hayden on the south side of Highway 40; a 134-mile stretch of the Yampa River, considered the heart of the state park; and the roughly 600-acre Elkhead Reservoir.

Yampa River State Park

The Yampa River supports a rich agricultural heritage that shapes the unique character of this area. One of the most hydrologically and biologically intact rivers in the West, the Yampa supports diverse and globally rare riparian plant communities, as well as a variety of native aquatic communities, including four federally-listed fish species—Colorado pikeminnow, humpback chub, bonytail chub, and razorback sucker—and candidate species such as the Colorado River cutthroat trout. This extensive river system also supports significant

bird species. Sandhill cranes stage on the Yampa River during migratory travel, and care for their young until they're ready to fly. Blue Heron rookeries coexist with nesting bald eagles and other avian species. This area of Northwest Colorado is also known for abundant big game species: elk, deer and antelope can be found throughout the year.

The state park's headquarters, located right on the Yampa River, feature a 1.25-mile nature trail with an observation deck, a visitor center, a sand volleyball court, and a playground. Excellent camping options also exist: 35 electric sites, 15 non-electrical sites, teepees, and group campsites.

The park's second component, a 134-mile stretch of the Yampa River, stretches from Hayden to the Dinosaur National Monument near the Utah border. Thirteen river access points offer recreationists many opportunities: day use/picnicking, six primitive camping areas, Class I-V river boating, and fishing from the river banks and on miles of flat water. Yampa anglers fish for both warm-water and cold-water species. Upstream of the park, you'll find one of the healthiest trout fisheries in the state. A variety of fishing opportunities exist in the Steamboat Springs area. On the eastern end of Yampa River State Park, from Hayden to Craig, fishing enthusiasts find trout, small-mouth bass, and northern pike, and on the western end of the river, from Craig to Maybell, is where you'll find warm-water species, including a good small-mouth bass fishery, northern pike, and catfish.

Elkhead Reservoir represents the third major component of the Yampa River State Park system. In addition to boating, fishing, swimming, and water skiing, visitors can enjoy new boat ramps, camping facilities, beaches, and restrooms. Drive about five miles west on Highway 40 from the Yampa River State Park headquarters and head north on the next major road, County Road 29. Visit *www.parks.state.co.us* for maps, a park brochure, and detailed information.

Elkhead Reservoir

Loudy Simpson Park

Moffat County
Craig

Loudy Simpson Park, situated south of Craig along the Yampa River, has a nine-hole disc golf course, a Kiwanis self-guided nature trail, an ADA-accessible fishing dock on a fishing lagoon, a boat launch for Yampa River access, more than three miles of walking trails, and camping and picnicking sites equipped with tables and BBQ grills. Take South Ranney Street south from Highway 40 in town, and look for the park on the right after you cross the Yampa River.

A prominent landmark located five miles northwest of Craig, **Cedar Mountain** encompasses 880-acres of Bureau of Land Management public land. With an elevation of 6,500 feet, Cedar Mountain rises 1,000 feet above the Yampa Valley, providing panoramic views. Because of its isolation from similar terrain, the horseshoe-shaped rim affords a superior view of the surrounding countryside. Great hiking trails and other year-round recreational opportunities are available. From Craig, take

Highway 40 west for one mile, and turn right on County Road 7. Go north five miles, and turn right on Cedar Mountain Access

Road/BLM Route #2190 (currently a steep dirt road only passable in good weather). *www.blm.gov*

Maybell

The town of Maybell west of Craig on Highway 40 is best known as the turnoff en route to a Yampa and Green River boating adventure. **Maybell Park** is always filled with campers coming and going from the river put-ins to the northwest. On the north side of the highway, it's hard to miss.

Rio Blanco County
Meeker

In the heart of White River country, Meeker serves as an entryway to some of the best hunting, fishing, hiking, and snowmobiling in Colorado. If you're with the kids, check out **Paintbrush Park's** playground and other facilities on the north side of town. Drive north on 3rd Street from Highway 13 to Garfield Street. Go right to Sulphur Creek Road, and north to the park on the right by the elementary school. *www.meekerrecdistrict.com*

Rangely

Located five miles east of Rangely along Highway 64 and the beautiful White River, **Kenney Reservoir** offers a wide variety of recreational facilities and leisure activities, including great fishing. The reservoir also features a marina and swimming area, as well as horseshoe pits, sand play areas, group shelters, and restrooms. The ADA-accessible facilities are all open in spring and summer. *www.rangely.com*

Paintbrush Park

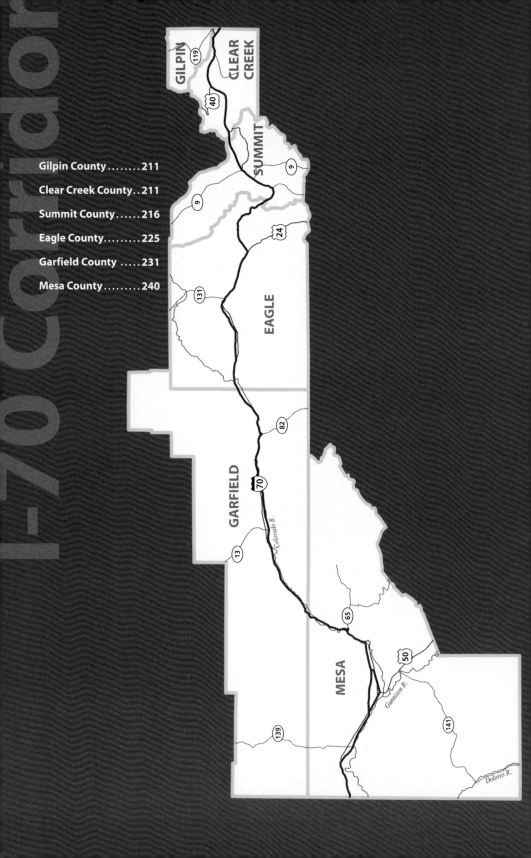

I-70 Corridor

Gilpin County

Golden Gate Canyon State Park lies in both Gilpin and Jefferson counties and encompasses more than 12,000 acres of dense forest, rocky peaks, and aspen-rimmed meadows laced with miles of trails. Hikers, horseback riders, mountain bikers, and winter sports enthusiasts flock to this incredible setting throughout the year. Only 30 miles from Denver, Golden Gate Canyon's amenities include electrical hook-ups and tent-sites in two different campgrounds, stocked fishing ponds, picnic sites, and the Panorama Point Scenic Overlook where visitors can see 100 miles of the Continental Divide. The park's numerous facilities can host events from weddings to family reunions and company picnics. Besides camping, overnight guests can also stay at one of Golden Gate's five cabins and two yurts. Winter finds visitors cross-country skiing, snowshoeing, sledding, ice fishing, and ice skating.

An abundance and variety of wildlife live in Golden Gate State Park, making it ideal for wildlife watching and photography. Large mammals include moose, bighorn sheep, black bear, mule deer, and elk. Smaller animals commonly spotted are snowshoe hare, coyote, bobcat, beaver, weasel, marten, fox, marmot, and porcupine. Binoculars will come in handy for viewing the park's many bird species such as blue grouse, ptarmigan, golden eagle, bald eagle, Steller's jay, gray jay, chickadee, rosy finch, and several species of waterfowl. Anglers fish for brook trout, cutthroat trout, brown trout, rainbow trout, arctic grayling, and others. From Golden, take Highway 93 north one mile to Golden Gate Canyon Road. Turn left, and continue for 13 miles to the park. A variety of park maps can be found at *www.parks.state.co.us.*

Featuring ball fields and a playground, **Pete Gones Memorial Park** is Gilpin County's primary community park resource. You'll find it on the north side of Golden Gate Canyon Road, four miles past Golden Gate Canyon State Park.

Clear Creek County
Evergreen/Idaho Springs

Part of a 20-mile wildlife corridor between Elk Meadow in Jefferson County and Mount Evans in Clear Creek County, the **Beaver Brook Watershed** features meadows, bubbling brooks, forested slopes, abundant wildlife, and dramatic rock outcroppings. This area is among the most intact ecosystems in the Front Range, and is an essential link in a long wildlife corridor that includes other open space lands. Elk, deer, bear, turkey, and mountain lion are some of Beaver Brook's wildlife inhabitants. The watershed also supports a variety of rare plant species. Located just west of Evergreen, Beaver Brook is traversed by Highway 103, providing a popular scenic drive between Evergreen and Echo Lake.

As of this guidebook's publication, Clear Creek County Open Space was in the process of developing a management plan for the Beaver Brook Watershed. However, existing rules for the property allow only non-motorized recreation such as hiking, mountain biking on trails, snowshoeing, cross-country skiing, horseback riding, and picnicking. Dogs on leash are permitted (but not in the water), but overnight camping is not allowed. Beaver Brook Canyon Road provides the best access to the watershed. Exit I-70 at the

Floyd Hill/Beaver Brook Road Exit, and drive south to the T-intersection. Continue left on Beaver Brook Canyon Road past Clear Creek High School as you enter the canyon. When the road forks, take a left onto Pat Creek Road. The road ends at the gate into the watershed where a few parking spaces are located. For current information, visit *www.co.clear-creek.co.us.*

The **Greenway Project** is a major undertaking in Clear Creek County's open space plan. The envisioned greenway would run alongside Clear Creek, between Jefferson County and the Continental Divide. This tract of land would link communities with a string of open spaces, parks, recreational facilities, and commercial recreation providers. The project aims to embrace the county's unique cultural heritage and natural environment, and provide a comprehensive resource for families, visitors, and outdoor enthusiasts.

Clear Creek County's 76-acre **Oxbow Parcel** will be incorporated in the Greenway Project. The property adjoins Jefferson County Open Space land (Clear Creek Park) to the east and existing Clear Creek County open space to the south. The Oxbow Parcel is located just west of the Jefferson County line, one-half mile upstream on Highway 119. Tracks for the Colorado Southern Railroad between Golden and Silver Plume, which followed Clear Creek around the oxbow, were removed in 1941. When U.S. Highway 6 was constructed in the 1950s, a tunnel was cut through the ridge, leaving the oxbow isolated and quiet—a significant step in protecting what is unique bighorn sheep habitat. A bike path will be constructed along the old railroad grade, providing a link that will one day be part of a path extending all the way through Clear Creek Canyon from Golden to Idaho Springs and beyond. Oxbow's rafting, Cat Slab rock climbing, fishing opportunities, and abundant wildflowers offer more ways to enjoy the canyon. *www.co.clear-creek.co.us*

Scott Lancaster Memorial Bike Path descends two miles along Clear Creek from Idaho

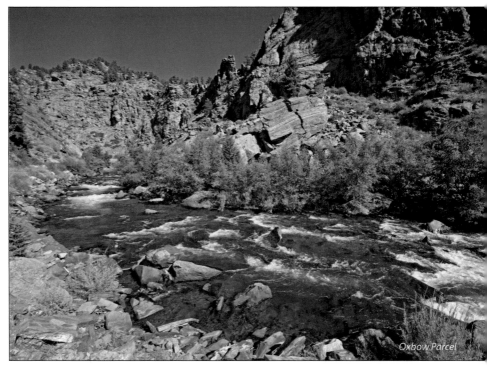

Oxbow Parcel

Springs to Kermit's Bar at the intersection of I-70 and Highway 6. In Idaho Springs, travel east on Colorado Boulevard over I-70 to County Road 314. Follow 314 east to its end at the trailhead.

Georgetown

Georgetown has preserved its mining heritage better than any other 19th century town in Colorado. After riding the Georgetown-Silver Plume Loop Railroad, why not take the kids fishing or to one of the town's parks? You can tell that a lot of love, creativity, and imagination went into building **Foster's Place Playground,** built by the community in memory of a young Georgetown child who passed away. The architecture and attention to detail is just amazing. It's at the intersection of 10th and Park Streets. **Georgetown Lake** has great year-round fishing, even through the ice!

Georgetown Lake

Summit County
Silverthorne

Silverthorne's paved **Blue River Trail** provides the perfect route for experiencing the Blue River and its scenic surroundings. On foot or bike, with or without a fishing pole (the Blue River is world-famous for its trout fishery), this family-friendly trail follows the river as it winds through Silverthorne. The Blue River Trail is relatively flat through town, but if you're looking for a workout with significant elevation gain, hop on a section at the town's south end and start climbing the switchbacks up to Dillon Reservoir. Continuing from Highway 9, past the Silverthorne Pavilion, and up to Silverthorne's Town Hall, this section of the Blue has it all for the fishing enthusiast: waterfalls with pools, strategically-placed boulders, and J-hook structures. Public access ends on the west side of the river, just north of the Forest Service building. Public access continues on the east side of the river in the form of a dirt path, and is accessible from the paved recreation path. *www.silverthorne.org*

Silverthorne Skate Park in **Rainbow Park** at 430 Rainbow Drive is a great resource for kids. Take 6th Street east from Highway 9, and bear right on Center Circle to Rainbow Drive. *www.silverthorne.org*

Cow Camp Open Space was once a working ranch that the Summit County Open Space and Trails Department acquired. The approximately 925-acre property is located in the Lower Blue River Valley at the north end of Green Mountain Reservoir, north and east of Highway 9 in the foothills of the

This Project Funded In Part By

Great Outdoors Colorado

Through Funds From

The Colorado Lottery

Bill Owens.
GOVERNOR OF COLORADO

DON'T TREAD ON ME

GREAT OUTDOORS
COLORADO

COLORADO
LOTTERY

Conservation Easement Held by
CONTINENTAL DIVIDE
www.CDLT.org

Williams Fork Mountains. The property is mostly open and covered in sage and meadow grasses, with beautiful wildflowers blooming May through August. Views of Green Mountain Reservoir and the Gore Range/Eagles Nest Wilderness are spectacular. You'll find a makeshift parking area on the north side of Highway 9, about one half mile north of the Cow Creek Campground road. Park here, look for the open space sign, and enter the gate to access the property. Only foot traffic is allowed.

Also managed by Summit County Open Space, **Doig Meadow Open Space** has simi-

lar characteristics as Cow Camp. The northwest corner of the property is elevated and affords lovely views of the Green River and Gore Range, as well as the Williams Fork Mountains to the east. It's located on the south end of Green Mountain Reservoir north of Highway 9. Immediately north of Heeney Road, Highway 9 crosses the Blue River. You'll see a road on the right and the sign for Blue River State Wildlife Area. Take this road east, and look for the parking areas. All of the land to the north of the road is Doig Meadow Open Space and is accessible on foot.

Bashore Open Space

Bashore Open Space, located within the Wildernest Subdivision southwest of Silverthorne, is marked by wetlands, lodgepole pine forest, and beautiful wildflowers that bloom in the summer. Most of the open land between the homes along Royal Buffalo Drive to the north and Wildernest Road to the south is protected. Parking along these roads is limited, and you need to be aware of private property. Bashore is also managed by the Summit County Open Space Department. *www.co.summit.co.us*

Dillon

Swan Mountain Recreation Path connects the Keystone/Snake River Basin and Breckenridge/Upper Blue Basin areas, and also serves to complete the popular paved trail that circles

Dillon Reservoir. The path offers stunning views of the mountains and ranges that define the aptly-named Summit County. The Summit County Recreational Pathway System, aka recpath, is a 55-mile network of paved, non-motorized pathways that connects towns and resorts throughout Summit County. The trail system also connects to Eagle via Vail Pass. Information and maps are available at www.co.summit.co.us and *www.summitbiking.org.*

Considered one of the area's best-kept secrets, **Dillon Nature Preserve** offers a peaceful escape for those wanting an easy walk through woodlands. The preserve's two loop trails—the shorter Meadow Trail Loop and the more scenic Ridge Trail Loop—were built in 1999 by Volunteers for Outdoors Colorado. Ideal for hiking, snowshoeing, and cross-country skiing, the trails feature overlooks, rest benches, and many other opportunities to take in incredible views. You'll also find interpretive signage—designed and written by Dillon Valley Elementary 5th graders—about the trees, wildlife, and native plants in the preserve, and the area's history. Bicycles are prohibited on the trail system, but dogs are allowed on-leash.

Dillon Nature Preserve is located on the Roberts Tunnel Peninsula, to the right of Highway 6 and just past Lake Dillon if you're traveling towards Keystone. To access the preserve, use the designated parking lot on the west side of Highway 6, across from the historic Dillon cemetery and west of the Summerwood Subdivision. From the parking area, head west to the paved recpath. Following the path briefly to the peninsula signboard and map, take the dirt road one-half mile with Lake Dillon and the Gore Range to your right; you'll be directly across the inlet from the Dillon Marina. At this point, you'll leave the dirt road, and the trail will take you up a hill through a meadow. At the top of the hill, you can take a right onto the Ridge Trail Loop. *www.townofdillon.com*

The meadows at **Iron Springs Open Space** bloom profusely with wildflowers in summer, and the views of Lake Dillon are lovely. Managed by Summit County's Open Space Department, Iron Springs is located in the Upper Blue Basin along Highway 9, approximately two miles east of the Town of Frisco

overlooking Dillon Reservoir, and north of the Summit High School campus. The Summit County recpath, connecting Breckenridge and Frisco, provides the primary public access to the property as well as Iron Springs Road, which is not open to motorized traffic. On the southwest corner of Lake Dillon across from the property, a gravel area exists within the right-of-way on the east side of Highway 9. People often park here to access Iron Springs Road. Just walk across the highway to the dirt road on the other side. Iron Springs Open Space is all the land to the north of the road. Foot access only.

Iron Springs Open Space

French Creek Trail

Breckenridge

The Town of Breckenridge's extraordinary trail system winds through natural and historical scenery that is a byproduct of its mining heritage. The French Gulch area contains many miles of natural-surface trails for bikers and hikers, two of which are the **French Creek** and **Turks Trails**. For complete information and a great map, visit *www.townofbreckenridge.com*.

The 156-acre **Cobb and Ebert Placer Open Space,** aka Upper French Gulch, is located in the Upper Blue Basin of Summit County, two miles east of Breckenridge town limits. Managed by the Summit County Open Space and Trails Department, the property straddles French Gulch and includes one of the last intact montane riparian willow carr wetlands in the Upper Blue Basin. It has been identified as one of the most ecologically-significant portions of the Golden Horseshoe, an 8,600-acre backcountry area immediately northeast of Breckenridge, valued for its open

McCullough Gulch Open Space

Cobb and Ebert Placer Open Space

space, wildlife habitat, and recreational trail system. Intact mining structures in the area are remnants of Breckenridge's 19th-century mining heritage. Two county roads, French Gulch Road and Sallie Barber Road, pass through the property, providing public access to miles of backcountry trails on the adjacent Arapahoe National Forest. Breckenridge trail maps are useful in accessing this open space.

The tiny seven-acre **McCullough Gulch Open Space** is located six miles south of Breckenridge, along the west side of the Highway 9 right-of-way. To the east of the highway is the Skier's Edge Lodge, and to the north lies the privately owned 20-acre McCullough Gulch wetlands complex. McCullough Creek runs through this small but strategic prop-

erty, which provides public access to National Forest lands and protects critical wildlife habitat. Look for the parking area across Highway 9 from Skier's Edge.

The **Gold Run Nordic Center** features 22 km of groomed classic and skate-ski trails, 10 km of snowshoe trails, free pond ice-skating, horse-drawn sleigh rides, ski lessons for all abilities, and a clubhouse restaurant. With ideal terrain for novices, miles upon miles of intermediate trails, challenging routes for advanced skiers, and 10 km of snowshoe trails, Gold Run promises fun for everyone. Take Tiger Road east from Highway 9 to Clubhouse Drive. Make a right to the center at 200 Clubhouse Drive. *www.townofbreckenridge.com*

Eagle County
Vail

The **Betty Ford Alpine Gardens** is a stunning mountain garden set in the shadow of the breathtaking Gore Range. The gardens' perennial beds, rock gardens, and waterfalls

display an astonishing collection of the world's most unique and beautiful high-elevation plants. With every color and species imaginable and accessible, the photographic possibilities are limitless—without having to backpack for miles!

The gardens' education programs for children run from mid-June through mid-August. Hands-on learning is an integral part of each program, all of which are intended for children ages 5-10, although exceptions are made. Kids' classes meet in the Children's Garden Amphitheater, which serves as an outdoor classroom and a gathering space for both kids and adults. The surrounding garden, representative of the natural landscape adjacent to Gore Creek in Vail Village, features solstice stones that frame sunrise and sunset at summer and winter solstice. Adult education programs are also available.

From east or west on I-70, take Exit 176, the main Vail exit, and go under the highway to the second roundabout. Travel east on South Frontage Road past the stop sign, and you'll see the tennis courts and softball fields at Ford Park on your right. Betty Ford Alpine Gardens are located at 530 South Frontage Road in Ford Park. Park in the lot next to the softball fields or tennis courts, and follow the asphalt path to the gardens. *www.bettyfordalpinegardens.org*

Eagle-Vail

If you're driving along I-70 west of Vail in the heat of summer, consider cooling off in the **Eagle-Vail Outdoor Lap and Leisure Pool.** Take the westbound I-70 Eagle-Vail Exit onto Highway 6. Head west to the first left at Eagle Road and drive east to Eagle Drive. The pool is on your right. *www.eaglevail.org*

Minturn

As an alternative to somewhat pricey Vail, the town of Minturn (pronounced "Min-urn" by locals) offers inexpensive lodging and dining options. **Little Beach Park and Amphitheater** is tucked between the Minturn cliffs and the Eagle River, a delightful and scenic location for a family picnic. The park features lots of shade trees, picnic tables, and grills, a variety of play structures for children, and easy access to the river. To get to the park, make a left on Ballpark/Cemetery Road just outside of downtown Minturn. *www.minturn.org*

Avon/Edwards

The Western Eagle County Metropolitan Recreation District strives to provide western Eagle County with high-quality, affordable recreational activities and facilities for youth and adults. Encompassing an estimated 840 square miles in Eagle County, the district serves the communities of Eagle, Edwards, Gypsum, Bond, McCoy, Cordillera, Lake Creek, and Wolcott. *www.townofeagle.org*

Eagle Valley Trail

Eagle Valley Trail is an ambitious effort to create a continuous 63-mile paved trail from Vail to Dotsero, effectively following the magnificent Eagle River. As of this book's publication, 33 miles were complete. One of my favorite stretches connects the communities of Avon and Edwards. See maps and information at *www.eaglecounty.us.*

Don't miss the **Freedom Skate Park and Spray Park** next to the field house in Edwards. Both provide exceptional opportunities for family fun, especially if you're driving I-70

and need a break. You'll also want to check out the rest of the complex, which offers miniature golf, batting cages, a 28-foot climbing

Sylvan Lake State Park

tower and bouldering wall, a full-service gymnastics center offering youth and adult classes, a 15,000-square-foot turf field, a flexible activity room featuring laser tag, a 10,000-square-foot multi-sport arena, and Human Dynamo Bikes that generate real-time electricity to help power the field house. From I-70, take Exit 163 south onto Edwards Village Boulevard, and look for the ball fields. *www.wecmrd.org*

Eagle

Make time for some contemplation at peaceful **Sylvan Lake State Park.** A gateway to the White River National Forest and the Holy Cross Wilderness, Sylvan offers quiet recreational opportunities such as non-motorized boating and non-electrical camping. Or, spend a few nights in a cabin or yurt while gazing at majestic mountains against the backdrop of a deep blue sky. Enjoy fishing, hiking, picnicking, nature study, photography, and boating (no motors except for electric trolling) in spring, summer, and fall. In winter, wake up to a fresh blanket of snow for a day of snowshoeing, cross-country skiing, ice fishing, or snowmobiling. Year-round,

this park offers folks a much-needed break from the daily grind.

The park is located in the White River National Forest, which provides ideal habitat for a variety of wildlife: red fox, marmots, mule deer, elk, black bear, pine marten, coyote, porcupine, cottontail rabbit, beaver, voles, and shrews are common inhabitants. Located at 8,500 feet, Sylvan boasts a diverse plant community. Aspen and coniferous forest occupies the slopes above the lake. Lodgepole pine and Douglas-fir are prevalent on the moist slopes, while ponderosa pine and Rocky Mountain juniper occupy drier slopes. Besides aspen, you'll find narrowleaf cottonwood, Colorado blue spruce and lodgepole pine, as well as a variety of wildflowers.

Visit the park the last two weeks of September for incredible autumn aspen photos. Your best options are from the north end of the park, through the park, and up and over Crooked Creek Pass on the way to Ruedi Reservoir. (See my other guidebook, *John Fielder's Best of Colorado,* for more information on this area.) Take I-70 to Eagle Exit 147. Turn south and follow signs through town. On the south side of town, turn south

Rock Bottom Ranch

on Brush Creek Road and travel 10 miles to the visitor center. Continue on Brush Creek Road until the road forks and becomes dirt. At the fork, stay right and travel five miles to the lake, campground, and cabins. *www.parks.state.co.us*

El Jebel

The hub for environmental education, wildlands preservation, and sustainable agriculture in the mid-Roaring Fork Valley, **Rock Bottom Ranch,** is also a 113-acre wildlife preserve that is run by the Aspen Center for Environmental Studies. Remotely located between the Roaring Fork River and the crown of Mount Sopris, the ranch is located midway between Basalt and Carbondale on the Rio Grande Trail. You'll find wetlands, spring-fed ponds, cottonwood bottomlands, a portion of the Roaring Fork River, and views of the pinyon juniper woodland on adjacent BLM land.

In 1999, the Aspen Center for Environmental Studies purchased a 113-acre parcel from the Cole family with an agreement to protect the property's important riparian habitat and broaden the center's educational and scientific outreach programs throughout the valley. A conservation easement on the property ensures that it will remain undeveloped, perpetually offering winter range and unobstructed river access for resident herds of elk and mule deer. By using minimal management practices, Rock Bottom Ranch helps enhance the biodiversity and ecological health of the land. This hands-off approach allows for heron, hawk, and owl nesting grounds, as well as habitat for wildlife including bear, coyote, bobcat, weasel, and beaver. In addition to the riparian corridor, another 28 acres of the ranch's wet meadows and sub-irrigated pastures have been restored to valuable wetland habitat. Along with providing grasses to wintering ungulate herds, these meadows provide nesting grounds for Wilson's Snipes, as well as red-winged and yellow-headed blackbirds.

Rock Bottom Ranch is open to the public from 9 a.m. to 5 p.m., Monday through Saturday, in the summer months, and Monday through Friday in the winter months. Take a guided tour of the farmyard, walk down its nature trail, peruse the library, or picnic on Cole Island. If driving from Carbondale on Highway 82, turn right onto Willits Lane just past El Jebel. Then turn right onto Hooks Lane and cross the Roaring Fork River. After the bridge, take an immediate right onto Hooks Spur Road, which dead ends at Rock Bottom Ranch. *www.aspennature.org*

Basalt Riverfront Park

Basalt

The **Basalt Riverfront Park** lies along the banks of the Roaring Fork River just west of downtown Basalt. The park and open space provide a scenic area for local artists and photographers, river recreation, fishing in Gold Medal waters, and picnicking opportunities. This area also enhances and protects the wetlands where waterfowl and other wildlife thrive. You'll find the park next to the popular Taqueria el Nopal Mexican restaurant. There's great Basalt shopping, too! *www.basalt.net*

Garfield County
Carbondale

Extending 5.2 miles, the first leg of the **Crystal Valley Trail** bike trail lies on the east side of Highway 133 along a stretch of the beautiful Crystal River. For most of the trail, the eight-foot-wide asphalt trail is complemented with an additional four feet of soft surface for equestrians and other users. Park at the Roaring Fork High School lot south of Carbondale to begin the 10-mile round trip. Bring your camera! The photographs of Mount Sopris, the Crystal River, and bucolic

Crystal Valley Trail

Promenade Park

ranch meadows are as stunning as any place in Colorado. *www.aspenpitkin.com*

A lovely little park with a gazebo and native plants, **Promenade Park** lies in downtown Carbondale at Colorado Avenue and North 4th Street at the Rio Grande Trail (see page 263 for Rio Grande Trail in Pitkin County). From Main Street, head north on 4th Street to the park on the left.

Glenwood Springs

South Canyon Trail is part of a Garfield County initiative to connect Glenwood Springs with Mesa County to the west via a 47-mile-long trail along the Colorado River. This portion is accessible by a trailhead located at the start of the South Canyon Creek Road. Take Exit 111 south from I-70. *http://lovatrails.org*

New Castle

Located along the south side of the Colorado River, the 12-acre **Grand River Park** provides public access to 3,340 feet of the river. There's plenty to do at New Castle's newest park, which features a regulation soccer field,

Grand River Park

South Canyon Trail

playground, river beach, and half-mile trail with interpretive signs. A pond at the park has been expanded in an effort to improve habitat for the Northern Leopard Frog, a species of concern for the Colorado Division of Parks and Wildlife. Take the I-70 New Castle Exit south across the Colorado River. Go east on County Road 335, then left through the condos to the park. *www.newcastlecolorado.org*

The nearly three-acre **Alder Park** contains two micro soccer fields (half of regulation size), several trails, a pond, and large parking area. The park is located adjacent to Alder Avenue in the Castle Valley Ranch area. Take the I-70 Exit north across Highway 6 to Castle Valley Boulevard. Proceed west to Alder Avenue. Turn right and the park will be on your left. *www.newcastlecolorado.org*

Rifle

The crystal waters of **Rifle Gap State Park's** 350-acre reservoir offer superb fishing, swimming, water skiing, and boating. The long, narrow reservoir is popular with jet skiers and power boaters, and lake conditions are often ideal for sailing and windsurfing. Rifle Gap's clean waters and swim beach on the west side of the reservoir draws swimmers and waders as weather permits. Anglers fish for rainbow and German brown trout, walleye, pike, smallmouth and largemouth bass, and yellow perch. In winter, Rifle Gap offers Coloradans a premier ice-fishing destination. The park has 89 camping sites, with day-use activities and opportunities for picnicking. Check current boating, fishing and other conditions before making plans. Take I-70 to Exit 90/Rifle, and

then go north on Highway 13 for four miles. This takes you through Rifle on Railroad Avenue. When the road comes to a Y, stay to the right on Highway 13. Turn right onto Highway 325, and you'll see Rifle Gap about six miles down the road. *www.parks.state.co.us*

Photographers and movie crews from around

Alder Park

Rifle Falls State Park

the country come to **Rifle Falls State Park** to capture the park's lush vegetation, waterfalls, and unique scenery. The spray of the cascading triple waterfall ensures that surrounding trees and greenery are moist and plentiful. Intriguing limestone caves beneath the falls entice spelunkers and other visitors to explore their dark depths. Picnicking near the falls is also very popular. There's lots to see and do here, so spend a night or two in one of the 13 drive-in and seven walk-in campsites located to the south of the park along East Rifle Creek. To reach Rifle Falls State Park, use the directions for Rifle Gap State Park, and continue another four miles north on Highway 325. *www.parks.state.co.us*

Centennial Park

Rifle Creek Trail

An oil and gas boomtown, Rifle works hard to maintain a strong sense of community. **Deerfield Regional Park** contains open space along Rifle Creek, basketball courts, four softball fields, two soccer fields, the lighted Cooper Baseball Field, a picnic shelter, and playground. Take the Rifle/Highway 13 Exit north from I-70, and continue north on Highway 13/Railroad Avenue through town to 30th Street. Turn right into the park. You can access the north end of Rifle Creek Trail by turning south from Deerfield Park on Acadia Avenue. You'll see the trail on the left as you enter the neighborhood. Located on the south end of **Rifle Creek Trail** between 3rd and 9th Streets, **Centennial Park** features a sprayground water feature, picnic shelters, and open space. From Railroad Avenue, drive west on 5th Street to its terminus at the park. *www.rifleco.org*

At an elevation of 8,000 feet, **Vega State Park's** high-mountain lake sits in a beautiful meadow on the western edge of Grand Mesa National Forest. I love the reflection photos at sunrise. A year-round recreationist's haven,

Deerfield Regional Park

Vega features fishing, boating, water skiing, birding, ice fishing, cross-country skiing, and hiking. Snowmobilers and off-highway vehicle riders can also access hundreds of miles of trails in Grand Mesa National Forest. Anglers especially enjoy the cold-water fishing opportunities, which include rainbow, cutthroat, cutbow, and brook trout. Ospreys are often spotted using the platforms installed on the edge of the lake to feed on the fresh trout.

Four campgrounds surround the lake, with 109 campsites that range from pull-throughs with electric hookups to 10 walk-in tent sites in the Pioneer Campground.

Vega also offers year-round rental of five cozy cabins, which accommodate up to six people and are located adjacent to a sledding hill. To escape the crowds, reserve a cabin mid-week. From Grand Junction, take Exit 49 off I-70 to Highway 65. Go about 18 miles, and turn left onto Highway 330. Then proceed about 24 miles to the town of Collbran. Stay on 330 east past Collbran for about eight miles to Mesa County Road 64 6/10ths Road (no joke!). Then turn right at the Vega State Park sign. Go five miles to the park entrance station. To reach the visitors' center, go another half mile and turn right across Vega Dam. *www.parks.state.co.us*

Mesa County
Palisade

Tilman Bishop State Wildlife Area is a pretty little valley near the orchard town of Palisade. The fishing, wildlife watching, and deer, waterfowl, and small game (except turkey) hunting at Tilman are superb. Public access is prohibited during the nesting and migrating period from March 15 through July 15, but the fall colors in October are lovely. Dogs are also prohibited except as hunting aids. From Palisade, take Highway 6 east, cross the Colorado River, and turn right (south) onto 38 Road. Travel up 38 Road onto East Orchard Mesa, where the road turns to the west and becomes F Road. When the road makes another 90 degree turn to the

south, proceed straight, make an immediate right after crossing the canal, and follow the canal road to the parking area. *www.wildlife. state.co.us/landwater/statewildlifeareas*

Located at the southeast corner of Palisade Park, **Riverbend Park** commemorates the late Congressman Wayne N. Aspinall, a state legislator and former Palisade resident, who advocated for the development of natural resources and reclamation projects. Big, beautiful deciduous trees define both parks, which are situated along the banks of the Colorado River. Take the main Palisade exit south from I-70 to Highway 6/West 8th Street. Go west to Brentwood Drive and south to the park. *www.townofpalisade.org*

Grand Junction

The Colorado River, and its confluence with the Gunnison River, defines Grand Junction as much as the backdrop of Colorado National Monument's red rocks. The wetlands, wildlife, and trees that change color from season to season are amazing. Reflection photos are everywhere. I especially enjoy photographing the trees in early May when the leaves are lime green, and in late October when they turn a brilliant orange. It's hard to escape the river while touring the city.

A collaboration of several local organizations, the Colorado Riverfront Greenway Partnership enhances and preserves the Colorado and Gunnison River corridors in Mesa County. The partnership's many achievements include constructing riverside parks, recreational trails, and public wildlife viewing areas, as well as protecting wildlife habitat and agricultural lands. Mesa Land Trust's involvement in the partnership has been focused on protecting wildlife habitat and farmlands through conservation easement acquisitions along the Colorado River corridor. You'll find many miles of multi-use trails along the Colorado River, which are managed by either the city or the Division of Parks and Wildlife.

Riverbend Park

Colorado River State Park was renamed **James M. Robb Colorado River State Park** in 2005 to honor the vision of Robb, who was instrumental in establishing the park and the "string of pearls" that comprise it. He and I served together in the early years on the board of Great Outdoors Colorado. It's tough to beat the incredible holdings of this state park. From Fruita on the west end, to Island Acres on the east end, the park is split into five sections consisting of uniquely different river- and lake-based outdoor recreation opportunities.

Birders at Colorado River State Park use the trails and overlooks to view abundant riparian and upland bird species. Bald eagles hunt over the river's open waters in the winter, and great blue heron rookeries can be seen adjacent to the park. The park is home to a variety of migratory and resident birds, including raptors, waterfowl, shorebirds, and grassland species such as lark and vesper sparrows, horned lark, and western meadowlark. If you're lucky, you'll spot red-tailed hawk, bald and golden eagles, osprey, swallows, hummingbirds, black-crowned night

Island Acres Section

Corn Lake Section

heron, ring-necked pheasant, quail, or wild turkey. Wildlife is also abundant along the riparian corridors.

Descriptions of Colorado River State Park's five distinct sections follow, listed from east to west. You'll experience something different in each of these special "pearls."

As the Colorado River and other erosional forces shaped the canyon, a large island was left in the middle of the river—hence, the name **Island Acres Section.** The history of the canyon and its island reflects the ever-changing face of the West. I love photographing the setting sun here! Island Acres features convenient and attractive spots along the river or near the park's three lakes for fishing, camping, picnicking, and hiking. Lucky visitors sometime catch a glimpse of bighorn sheep in the canyon or wild horses, which make their home at nearby Little Bookcliffs Wild Horse Range. Located at Exit 47 on I-70 in the scenic Debeque Canyon, Island Acres is open year-round for camping and day-use activities.

A day-use only site, the **Corn Lake Section** serves as headquarters for Colorado River State Park and the Colorado Division of Parks and Wildlife's Rocky Mountain Region office. In addition to a launching site for boaters and rafters on the Colorado River, Corn Lake features a .9-mile hard-packed trail along the lake's shoreline, which is used

Connected Lakes Section

for hiking and biking, and also provides river and lake access for fishing. Picnic sites and restrooms here are ADA-accessible. You'll find Corn Lake at 32 Road and the Colorado River. Great reflection photos here, too!

The **Colorado River Wildlife Area Section** is located one mile west of Corn Lake on D Road. This section was created to replace wetlands lost during the time of the Grand Valley Salinity Control Project, an effort to reduce the amount of salinity in select areas. Although recreational opportunities here are limited because of an emphasis on protection and enhancement of wildlife and wetlands habitat, visitors can enjoy hiking, viewing wildlife, and environmental education activities.

A portion of the Colorado River Wildlife Area Section, referred to as the **Pear Park Trail** section, has been known as Pear Park since the 1880s when Grand Valley settlers planted and established orchards along the Colorado River near D Road and 27 1/2 Road. In the 1890s, land for sale in the vicinity of 30 and D Roads was specifically marketed for its orchard potential. Fast forward to 2005 when a mile of paved, multi-use trail was opened

to the public between 29 Road and 30 Road. This extra mile provided a total of more than three miles of trail stretching west from Corn Lake at 32 Road. Several small lakes in the Pear Park Trail section provide critical habitat for endangered fish. No fishing or boating of any kind is allowed, but you'll find plentiful hiking and wildlife viewing opportunities in this area.

Also a day-use site, the **Connected Lakes Section** can be accessed by travelling north and west on Power Road off Highway 340. Connected Lakes features a network of trails that traverse a series of reclaimed gravel pits, and other recreational opportunities such as fishing, picnicking, hiking, and bird watching. Also in Connected Lakes, the **Blue Heron Trail** follows the north side of the Colorado River for 1.85 miles along the Redlands Parkway and River Road, and is accessible from several locations. The trailhead north of the river off Redlands Parkway also provides river access with a boat ramp and parking. There's a good map at *www.riverfrontproject.org.*

The **Fruita Section** is the first state park travelers encounter as they journey into Colorado

Fruita Section

Blue Heron Trail

from I-70 west. Open year-round for camping and day-use activities, this section of the state park features magnificent views of both the Colorado National Monument and the Book Cliffs area. It also offers exceptional camping facilities, lake fishing, swimming, and boating, as well as lovely picnic sites, seasonal birding, a walkway along the Colorado River, and a large visitor center. Nearby you'll discover renowned mountain biking trails, dinosaur sites, and red rock hiking. The Fruita Section is located south of I-70 Exit 19 on Highway 340, adjacent to the Colorado River. *www.parks.state.co.us*

The 81.4-acre **Canyon View Park** is a perfect place to stretch your legs when traveling I-70. The large park contains an exceptional variety of recreational facilities: an inline roller hockey rink, a professional quality baseball field, four lighted softball fields, 12 soccer/multipurpose fields (one lighted), two

lighted basketball courts, two lighted sand volleyball courts, six tennis courts, two playgrounds, trails, and open space. The park also contains three picnic shelters and three restroom facilities. You'll find it on the west end of Grand Junction, just south of I-70 on the 24 Road Exit.

The 10-acre **Westlake Park and Skate Park** features a playground, walking path, nine-hole disc golf course, and open space. Located

Canyon View Park

Dinosaur Hill Interpretive Trail

on the west side of Grand Junction, go west on Orchard from North 1st Street to the park located at 125 West Orchard Avenue. *www.gjcity.org*

Fruita

Fruita and Grand Junction get hot in the summer, so cool down at the **Fruita Community Outdoor Pool** located at 324 North Coulson Street. Take the I-70 Fruita Exit north on Cherry Street to West Pabor Avenue. Turn west to Coulson, and go north to the pool on the right.

Little Salt Wash Park features several sports fields, including a nine-hole disc golf course. For a small park, Little Salt Wash offers a lot of recreational opportunities. Check it out

by exiting I-70 at Fruita Exit 19. Go north 0.4 miles on Cherry Street, and take a right at Ottley Avenue. Go 0.8 miles to Pine Street/ 18 Road, take a left, and go 0.3 miles north. You'll see the park on your left along Little Salt Wash (just past K-1/3 Road). *www.fruita.org*

Do dinosaurs fascinate your kids? If so, you must stop in Grand Junction, a key component of the so-called "Dinosaur Diamond" region of Eastern Utah and Western Colorado. Dinosaur Diamond is an area where hundreds of dinosaur species have been discovered—many concentrated in the Grand Junction area. Several museums, attractions, and programs in the area offer opportunities to learn more about these prehistoric creatures, including the one-mile **Dinosaur Hill Interpretive Trail.** Walk the trail to see bones of the stegosaurus, brachiosaurus, and other "terrible lizards." Located in the McInnis Canyons National Conservation Area and managed by the Bureau of Land Management, Dinosaur Hill Trail is open all year, weather permitting. Take the I-70 Fruita/Highway 340 Exit south on 340 for 1.5 miles to the trailhead on your left. *www.visitgrandjunction.com*

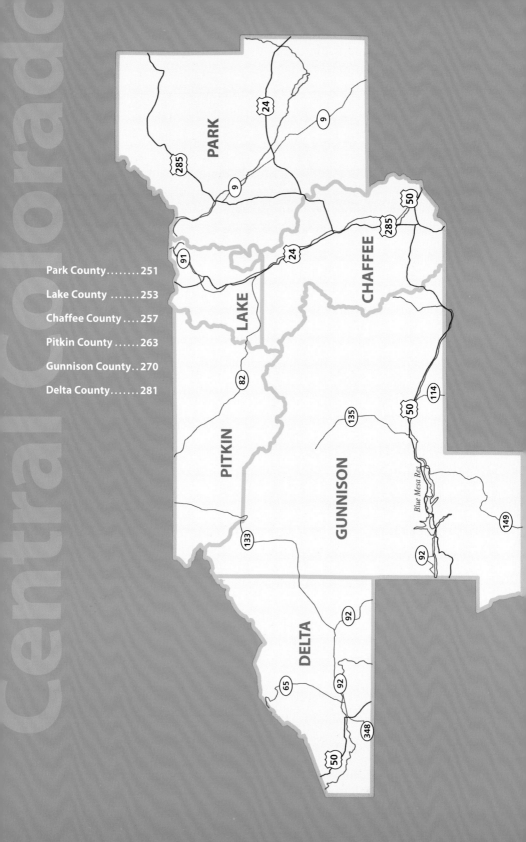

Central Colorado

PARK

285

24

9

9

50

285

91

24

CHAFFEE

LAKE

82

114

50

135

PITKIN

GUNNISON

Blue Mesa Res.

149

133

92

92

DELTA

65

92

348

50

Central Colorado

Park County

Fishing enthusiasts from around the world travel to South Park to fish its productive trout waters. Because they contain the highest quality aquatic habitat and offer the greatest potential for angling success in Colorado, more than 50 miles of public streams in this area have been designated Gold Medal trout waters by the Colorado Division of Parks and Wildlife. This designation doesn't come without a cost: These waters are some of the most widely-publicized and heavily-fished streams in the state. Although other waters in South Park are equally productive, they aren't generally open to the public. Due to the innovation of the South Park Fly Fishers program, however, this is changing. Several historic ranches have been secured for limited public fly fishing (for a daily fee) through the **South Park Fly Fishing** program. Because these lands are working cattle ranches, users must respect the wishes of each owner to ensure their continued availability. Since 2002, Park County has secured fishing leases on at least eight different ranches in South Park. The majority of each rod fee is given to the participating rancher, with the balance used to manage each property that is part the program. Thanks to the efforts of many partners, a considerable amount of stream habitat and historic structures have been preserved on the leased properties. Besides the availability of miles of private trout streams, some of the property leases also offer overnight lodging. *www.parkco.us* and *www.southparktrout.com*

Tarryall Notch Ranch, Park County

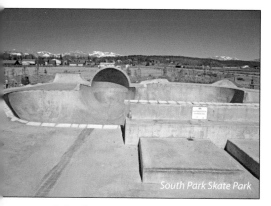

South Park Skate Park

Bailey

An outdoor museum along the banks of the South Platte River in downtown Bailey, **McGraw Park** features Entriken Cabin (the only surviving building from the original town of Bailey), Shawnee School, a Keystone railroad bridge, and several other period artifacts from the local area. McGraw Park is maintained and preserved by the Park County Historical Society. *www.parkcountyheritage.com*

Fairplay

Visit the **South Park Skate Park** at Fairplay's Recreation Center. From the only traffic light in town located at the intersection of Highways 9 and 285, go a little less than a mile north on 285, and take a left on County Road 3. You'll see the skate park on the left at 1190 Bullet Road. *www.thecoloradoskateboardguide.com.* You'll find a nice playground at Cohen Park, as well as the same amazing mountain views that surround the rest of Fairplay. **Cohen Park** is located north of Main Street at 8th and Clark Streets. *www.southparkrec.org*

Alma

Alma Playground, Park, and Riverwalk lie along the banks of the Middle Fork of the South Platte River in this historic 19th-century mining town, located north of Fairplay on Highway 9.

Cohen Park

Lake County
Leadville

Lake County Community Park is a great place to take the kids. You'll love the playground's unobstructed views of Mount Massive, and the kids can burn some energy at the park's synthetic turf soccer field—the highest in the world! From downtown Leadville, go west on 6th Street to its end (where it meets McWethy Drive). The **Mineral Belt Trail** runs right by it. *www.lakecountyco.com*

Offering unparalleled views of the Sawatch and Mosquito Ranges, the Mineral Belt Trail is one of Colorado's highest and most spectacular paved pathways. The non-motorized, ADA-accessible trail loops the town of Leadville, traveling through aspen groves, conifer forests, wildflower meadows, and open vista sage parks. Approximately six miles of the 11.6-mile trail winds through Leadville's historic Mining District. Featuring several trailheads and access points, the trail caters to bicyclists, walkers, strollers, and in-line skaters. Wintertime recreationists appreciate the trail's snowcat-groomed surface, which accommodates freestyle and classic Nordic skiing, snowshoeing, and winter biking.

The Mineral Belt Trail takes full advantage of Leadville's cultural and historic resources as well as the adjacent Mining District. It integrates portions of the three major rail grades that served the district around the turn of the century. The trail's alignment parallels California Gulch, the site of Leadville's first gold strike and earliest settlement, and it cuts through the heart of the mineral belt that earned Leadville the moniker, "Colorado's Silver City." Traversing five peaks that are more than 10,000-feet-high—Fryer, Fairview, Carbonate, Iron and Rock Hills—the trail offers travelers some insight into the pioneering spirit and fortitude required to sustain a living in such alpine environments.—*Editorial courtesy of coloradoinfo.com.* Learn more about the history of the Mineral Belt Trail at *www. mineralbelttrail.com.* The Rails-To-Trails Conservancy also offers good information about this and other Colorado trails at *www.traillink.com.*

Mineral Belt Trail

Sangree M. Froelicher Hut

Located south of Leadville on Highway 24, **Hayden Meadows Recreation Area** lies at the northern end of the Arkansas Headwaters Recreation Area. The area features fishing opportunities, ADA-accessible interpretive trails, five wetland boardwalks, and two bridges surrounding a small reservoir along the Arkansas River. From Leadville, head south on US 24 about six miles, passing Crystal Lakes and the turnoff to CR 7, to a bridge where the highway crosses the Arkansas River. Just past the bridge, turn left at your first opportunity, into the parking lot for Hayden Meadows.

Built in 1998, the **Sangree M. Froelicher Hut** is one of 32 rental huts that are part of Colorado's 10th Mountain Division Hut Association. The hut was named in honor of Staff Sergeant Sangree Mitchell Froelicher, 1st Platoon, Company B, 1st Battalion, 86th Mountain Infantry, who was killed in action in Italy in 1945. Lying at an elevation of 11,700 feet, the hut sleeps 26 people. Locate the trailhead and parking on the north side of Highway 91 between mile markers 4 and 5, between Fremont Pass and Leadville. *www.huts.org*

Hayden Meadows Recreation Area

Chaffee County

The **Arkansas Headwaters Recreation Area** is known as one of the nation's most popular locations for whitewater rafting and kayaking on the Arkansas River—among the world's most commercially-rafted rivers. The recreation area follows the magnificent and unpredictable Arkansas River for 150 miles, from the historic town of Leadville, through the Sawatch mountain range and Colorado's tallest mountains, all the way down to Pueblo on the edge of Colorado's plains. Adventurous boaters will experience waters ranging from roaring Class IV and V rapids to milder Class II and III whitewater, which is ideal for beginner and family trips. On any spring or summer day, hundreds of private and commercial rafters and kayakers flock to the upper Arkansas River for the challenge of turbulent rapids or the calm of smoother

waters. Besides boating, outdoor enthusiasts will find plenty to do here, including fishing, hiking, camping, picnicking, wildlife watching, mountain biking, and rock climbing. Even gold-panning is popular along the shores, deep canyons, broad valleys and towering mountain peaks found within the upper Arkansas River Valley.

Unlike most state parks in Colorado, the Arkansas Headwaters Recreation Area doesn't have one set of driving directions due to its linear nature and impressive length. Although a number of highways and roads enter the valley, the Arkansas River essentially follows Highways 24, 285, and 50 from north to southeast. Along the way you'll find six basic campgrounds, numerous picnic areas, fishing and boating access points, and trail access. For more information, visit the visitor center in Salida (it's the brick building with a blue roof on the corner of G and Sackett Streets), or view a high-resolution map of the entire route and facilities at *www.parks.state.co.us*. For a good commercial website offering activities in the valley, visit *www.coloradoheadwaters.com*.

Buena Vista

With its four main whitewater structures, numerous eddies, and trails, the **Buena Vista River & Whitewater Park** is one of Colorado's premier whitewater parks. All of its features have been fine-tuned to optimize hydraulic performance and enhance the park for all who enjoy it. Why not give it a try? You'll find ample parking, changing rooms, boat ramps, trails, and access all along the west side of the river. If whitewater action isn't your thing, the park also offers the **Boulder Garden Rocks and Ropes Course** for kids and families. Children from 5 to 12-years-old will have fun practicing and developing their climbing skills on the massive installation of artificial rocks. You'll find it just east of the Buena Vista Community Center. Take East Main Street east from Highway 24 to all of these facilities. *www.buenavistacolorado.org*

Arkansas Headwaters Recreation Area

Boulder Garden Rocks and Ropes Course

Named for a local artist, the **Barbara Whipple Trail** is actually a grouping of several trails on the east side of the Arkansas River. Accessible from the Buena Vista River Park Bridge, the 1.3-mile loop trail starts out steep at the Arkansas River Trailhead, but soon levels off. Popular with hikers, the route can be lengthened by taking one of its various trail connections. Looking back across the valley offers amazing views of the Collegiate Peaks. Traveling through a pinyon forest, the trail branches to a portion of the old Midland Railroad grade. Several kiosks along the way provide current and historical information about the area. *www.buenavistaco.gov*

Buena Vista River & Whitewater Park

Salida

Shaded by lovely willow trees along the Arkansas River in Historic Downtown Salida, **Riverside Park** provides a prime venue for spectators. Because this spot in the river serves as a popular play area for kayakers, it's not uncommon to see a number of onlookers watching the acrobatics in the whitewater. At the main traffic light in downtown Salida, go toward Tenderfoot Mountain, aka "S" Mountain, and you'll see the park along the river. **Alpine Park Playground** is located at 5th and E Streets just south of downtown Salida. In addition to a playground, the park features lots of shade trees and offers a peaceful, quiet alternative when Riverside Park is bustling with water lovers. The Colorado Division of Parks and Wildlife funded the **Salida Greenway Trail** that runs west through most of town and starts at Riverside Park. Check out the parks and trail master plan map at *www.salidarec.com*.

Alpine Park Playground

Salida is known as one of America's best art towns. The **Salida Riverside Fine Arts Festival** is held every summer in August. *www.salidaartfestival.com*

Salida Greenway Trail

Poncha Springs

South Park Disc Golf Center, located on 20 acres south of Poncha Springs, is an amazing 18-hole course that winds through pinyon and juniper trees. Built to Professional Disc Golf Association standards, the free, public course is open year-round and frequented by "disc duffers" from around the country. Disc golf was formalized in the 1970s. The sport is similar to traditional golf, but instead of a ball and clubs, players use a flying disc (or Frisbee®). Like regular golf, the objective of disc golf is to complete each hole in the fewest number of strokes—or throws. Drive south on Highway 285 through Poncha Springs. Take the first left after crossing the South Fork of the Arkansas River on Hot Springs Road/County Road 115, and follow the signs to the course. *www.ponchaspringscolorado.us*

Rio Grande Trail

Pitkin County

Running 42.6 miles from Glenwood Springs to Aspen, the **Rio Grande Trail** is built within the former rail corridor of the Denver and Rio Grande Western Railroad's Aspen Branch. Train operations along this line ceased in phases between the 1960s and the mid-1990s, and in 1997 the rail corridor and track were obtained through a joint purchase. The asphalt-surfaced trail contains sections of both concrete and compacted travel, making it ideal for a variety of users, including pedestrians, bicyclists, in-line skaters, skateboarders, horseback riders, and people using wheelchairs. At various locations, you'll find picnic tables, benches, trash bins, and dog waste stations. Although no

restroom facilities or potable water are available, several spur trails lead to towns adjacent to the trail. During the winter months, the trail is plowed when snowfall exceeds three inches between Glenwood Springs and Main Street in Carbondale. Other sections are sometimes groomed for cross-country skiing. *www.aspennordic.com.* For general information, updates on trail conditions, and a great map of the entire trail, go to *www.rfta.com.* If you'd like to learn more about Colorado trails from the Rails-To-Trails Conservancy, visit *www.traillink.com.*

Aspen

Designers of the two-acre **Harmony Park** made impressive use of the neighborhood park's relatively tiny space. Features include a half-acre play lawn, age-separated play areas, naturalistic water features, native landscape zones, and large landforms that serve as sledding hills in the winter. In addition, ditch and storm water from neighborhood construction has been integrated into a water feature at the northern end of the park. Turn east on Stage Road just south of Aspen Airport to reach the park in the Burlingame neighborhood. *www.aspenpitkin.com*

Snowmass Village

Sky Mountain Park is comprised of the Seven Star Ranch, Droste, and Cozy Point open spaces, which constitute about 2,500 contiguous acres that have been protected in perpetuity. Features include five miles of singletrack trail on the ridge that lies west of Highway 82 and east of downtown Snowmass Village. Populated mostly by oak brush and sage, the ridge offers remarkable views of the Maroon Bells-Snowmass Wilderness to the west. When the oak trees turn orange and red in autumn, the color is quite amazing! You'll find trailhead parking on the south side of the ridge at the Buttermilk Ski Area parking lot, and on the north side of the ridge at the Snowmass Village Recreation Center and Town Park located at the inter-

Sky Mountain Park, Droste-Seven Star Open Space

section of Brush Creek and Highline Roads. *www.aspenpitkin.com*

Tom Blake Trail is one of many singletrack trails providing hiking and mountain biking access to Pitkin County's great network of open space properties. In this case, the view includes the gorgeous aspen in the White River National Forest. Located west of Sky Mountain Park, Tom Blake Trail's starting point is on the south side of Owl Creek Road near Mandalay Lane. There is no trailhead parking here, so it's best to access the trail from its other end at the Snowmass Village Mall. *www.singletracks.com*

Carbondale

Crystal Valley Trail is the first leg of what is hoped to be a 73-mile bike trail someday linking the towns of Carbondale, Redstone, and Crested Butte. Beginning at the Roaring Fork High School parking lot, this 5.2-mile paved stretch follows the beautiful Crystal River and Highway 133 west toward Redstone. Along most of the trail, where there is enough space, the eight-foot-wide trail is extended by an additional four feet of soft surface for equestrians and other users. You'll never lose sight of Mount Sopris at any point along the way! *www.aspenpitkin.com*

Tom Blake Trail

Droste-Seven Star Open Space

The **Carbondale Boat Ramp** allows anglers and other water enthusiasts to access one of Colorado's most popular stretches of river, the Roaring Fork. From southbound High-way 82 before the Carbondale Exit, turn right onto County Road 106, and bear left to its end at the ramp. You'll also find good access to the Rio Grande Trail.

Redstone

Filoha Meadows Open Space lies in the scenic Crystal River Valley. The pristine waters of the Crystal River run through the sun-exposed property; its vibrant meadows, wetlands, and ponds are warmed by geothermal activity, and the 1.5-acre Penny Hot Springs is locally famous for its soothing waters. Located two miles north of Redstone, Filoha Meadows is known for its stunning vistas—views so impressive that the Disney movie, *Tall Tales* was filmed here. To protect critical bighorn sheep and elk habitat, visitors are allowed access only along the historic rail bed that traverses the property east of the river, and only for three months of the year in July, August, and September from one-half hour after sunrise to one-half hour before sunset.

The combination of the hot springs and geothermal activity at Filoha—which means "hot water" in Ethiopian—creates a biologically-diverse community. The warm, rolling meadows remain snow-free, providing a winter range for bighorn sheep as well as elk, which are known to calve near the river in the spring. Beavers help create wetlands, and predators such as coyotes and foxes consider the meadows their hunting grounds. With both fresh water and hot, mineral spring-fed wetlands, rare plant communities thrive. At least three orchid species have been found on the property, including the stream orchid and canyon bog orchid, and more than 13 acres of beaked spikerush, which is rare not only in Colorado but also in the U.S. Steep hillsides and rocky cliffs contain Douglas fir, Gambel oak, and oceanspray, providing habitat for larger wildlife species and nesting sites for songbirds and blue grouse. Other wet meadows contain more common vegetation such as bulrushes, sedges, willows, and reedgrass, and the riverbanks on the southern half of the property are lined with cottonwoods and dense, diverse vegetation.

Open to the public year-round, Penny Hot Springs lies on the east side of Highway 133, on the west bank of the Crystal River. To access Filoha east of the Crystal, turn east off Highway 133 into Redstone. Turn left at the Redstone Art Center onto Redstone Road/County Road 3, and drive north past Redstone Campground. Bike or walk north

Filoha Meadows Open Space

out of Redstone to reach the property gate, but leave your bike at the gate. The Roaring Fork Conservancy often provides educational programs relating to Filoha, including guided walks to explore the property's rare population of fireflies. For more information, visit *www.roaringfork.org.*

Redstone Park lies between Highway 133 and Redstone Boulevard, just after you take the main Redstone Exit off the highway. On the left along the banks of the idyllic Crystal River, you'll see open space, flowers, trails, tables and benches for the perfect picnic.

Jorgensen Park

Gunnison County
Gunnison

The unique community of Gunnison, home of Western State College, offers several lovely parks and trails. **American Legion Memorial Park** has a nice playground, and it's located right across East Tomichi Avenue/Highway 50 from **Jorgensen Park** and Pac Man Pond. Both parks are on the east side of town at Teller Street and Tomichi. If you're a boater, you'll find a great put-in on the Gunnison River at **West Tomichi Riverway Park,** located on the west side of town. Head west on Tomichi Avenue from Highway 50, and bear north to Diamond Lane. You'll see the park on the left. A paved pedestrian/bicycle trail, the **Gunnison Bridge to Bridge Trail** follows the river north and south through town.

West Tomichi Riverway Park

Gunnison Bridge to Bridge Trail

Access it via County Road 38/Airport Road, which turns south off Highway 50 just west of the airport. *www.cityofgunnison-co.gov*

The 8,500-acre **Hartman Rocks Recreation Area** is managed by the City and County of Gunnison and the Bureau of Land Management. A unique formation of granite outcrops, boulders, and eroded hoodoo formations, the rec area offers 33 miles of four-by-four roads, 39 miles of motorcycle trails, and 40 miles of singletrack mountain biking trails, as well as hiking and running trails. Drive to the west end of Gunnison on Highway 50, and turn south on County Road 38/Gold Basin Road. Proceed 2.2 miles, and look for the right turn into Hartman Rocks. *www.gunnisoncrestedbutte.com*

A guest/dude ranch since the early 1960s, **Waunita Hot Springs Ranch** sits 10 miles west of the Continental Divide at an elevation of 8,946 feet. Gunnison National Forest land and summer pasture surrounds the ranch, which is protected from development via conservation easements. Originally home to the Ute Indians, the property was homesteaded in the late 1880s, and became famous for the hot springs at the turn of the century. For a time, Waunita Hot Springs was owned and operated by Dr. Charles Davis from Chicago, who brought his patients out to bathe in the healing waters. Drive west on Highway 50 over Monarch Pass to mile marker 176. Turn north on County Road 887 to the ranch. *www.waunita.com*

Hartman Rocks Recreation Area

The 1,600 acres of sagelands at **Miller Ranch State Wildlife Area** offer hunting, hiking, and wildlife viewing. From Gunnison, go north on Highway 135 for 2.7 miles. Turn left at Ohio Creek Road/County Road 730, and travel 6.1 miles. At County Road 7, turn left and travel .6 miles to the entrance sign. *www.wildlife.state.co.us*

Crested Butte/Mt. Crested Butte

Crested Butte's newest regional park, **Rainbow Park** offers a variety of amenities, including a large playground, soccer field, pavilion, pond, climbing boulder, and picnic tables. A scenic view bench at Rainbow Pond provides an opportunity to enjoy the beautiful reflection of Mt. Crested Butte, and the Rainbow Pavilion is a terrific space for picnics, BBQs, and other events. If you're

visiting in September and October, you might catch the high school soccer team, the Titans, battling it out on the Rainbow Park Soccer Field. Open sunrise to sunset every day, the park is located at 8th Street and Maroon Avenue. *www.crestedbutte-co.gov*

Peanut Lake is one of Colorado's most spectacular reflection lakes. I've been taking participants in my photography workshops there for many years to photograph Mount Crested Butte at sunrise and sunset. It's just northwest of downtown. Take Maroon Avenue west to 2nd Street. Go north three blocks to Butte Avenue, and turn left. This becomes the dirt Peanut Lake Road. In less than a mile, you'll see Peanut Lake on your right.

The Crested Butte Land Trust protects most of Peanut Lake and the Slate River Valley in which it lies. Formed in 1991, the land trust—which has preserved more than 5,000 acres of land in the area—considers the Slate River Valley a priority area because it drains into the Slate River Wetlands Preserve, offers amazing views of Paradise Divide, and is located close to the Town of Crested Butte. A picturesque example of Crested Butte's iconic landscape, the wetlands preserve extends almost seven miles along the Slate

Peanut Lake

River and five miles along Washington Gulch. It encompasses 1,795 pristine acres north and south of town, including all of the natural wetland areas between the confluences of the Slate River and Baxter Gulch, and the Slate River and Oh-Be-Joyful Creek. (The Crested Butte Land Trust has preserved approximately 1,000 of these acres.)

The 80-acre Peanut Lake property includes 80 percent of Peanut Lake, extensive wetlands, and 1,400 feet of the Slate River. Purchased in 1996, the land is home to elk, deer, red and silver fox, ermine, beaver, and other wildlife, as well as an abundant bird population. In addition, at least 43 varieties of native vegetation are found here.

The 384-acre **Kochevar Parcel** is located on Smith Hill above the Slate River Valley. The Crested Butte Land Trust worked with the Trust for Public Land and the Kochevar family to permanently protect and preserve this acreage. Contiguous to the more than 1,200

acres that the Crested Butte Land Trust already holds in the area, the Kochevar Parcel connects four existing open space parcels, buffers National Forest land, preserves wildlife habitat (including an elk migration corridor), and provides future trail and recreation opportunities. More than 100 acres of the parcel are adjacent to and very visible from Crested Butte, and protecting this land preserves views of Paradise Divide. Currently, visitors can access the Kochevar Parcel only via mountain bike through the Saddle Ridge development (where no vehicle parking is allowed). By bike, ride the Gothic Road from Crested Butte past the Slate River Road. Take the next left into Saddle Ridge to the trail. *www.cblandtrust.org*

Whether spring, summer, or fall, the **Lower Loop Trail** offers a beautiful hike or mountain bike experience above Peanut Lake. The summer wildflowers are absolutely amazing! Once closed to the public because it crossed

Kochevar Parcel

Lower Loop Trail

private property, the Lower Loop Trail is now accessible because of the Crested Butte Land Trust's efforts. With little elevation change and an out-and-back distance of nine miles, this moderate mountain bike ride will take you an hour or two. See your options for reaching the Lower Loop Trail by looking at maps, descriptions, and at the Crested Butte Mountain Biking Association website. *www.cbmba.org.* Also, see information about this and other Colorado trails from the Rails-To-Trails Conservancy. *www.traillink.com.*

Slightly more than two miles in length, the paved **Mt. Crested Butte Recreation Path** connects the towns of Mt. Crested Butte and Crested Butte. Winding along the east side of Gothic Road and surrounded by beautiful pastures, meadows, wetlands, and vistas, the pedestrian/bike path features a series of interpretive plaques that provide information on the geology, history, and biology of the area. *www.mtcrestedbuttecolorado.us*

Big Mine Ice Arena is an NHL-size ice rink offering public skating and competitive ice hockey. Named after Crested Butte's historic Big Mine, formerly located next door, the ice arena's construction includes some of the old bricks from the mine's coke ovens. The arena is located at 2nd Street and Whiterock Avenue. *www.crestedbutte-co.gov*

Delta County

Delta

Located within the city limits of Delta near the confluence of the Gunnison and Uncompahgre Rivers, the 256-acre **Confluence Park** offers an abundance of recreational opportunities. The park's 60-acre lake allows non-motorized boating, has a boat ramp and dock on the northeast side of the lake, and an accessible fishing dike. In the summer, you can fish from the instructional pond, also on the park's north side, and skate on it in the winter. Summertime also sees lots of activity on the swim beach and the volleyball court, which are located on the west side of the lake. A five-mile pedestrian/bicycle trail meanders through the property, providing plenty of opportunities for viewing wildlife in natural habitats. Bird watchers will especially enjoy the bird sanctuary between the river and the lake. The park also includes an inline skate hockey rink. On the north side of town, from Highway 50 take Gunnison River Drive west to the park. *www.deltacountycolorado.com*

Special Events Arbor Council Tree Powwow at Confluence Park

Orchard City

Orchard City Public Park, aka **Field of Dreams,** has several baseball, softball, and soccer fields, a regulation basketball court, 1.5-mile walking path, pavilion, and a large playground. Visit this lovely facility the next time you're touring the farm and orchard country south of Grand Mesa. Drive east from Delta on Highway 92, and turn north on Highway 65 to Orchard City. Then travel less than a mile south on 2100 Road to the park. *www.orchardcityco.org*

Cedaredge

To reach Cedaredge Skate Park, go past Orchard City on Highway 65. When you get

North Fork Swimming Pool

to Cedaredge, head east on SE High Country Drive. Turn right at the huge sign with a skateboard on it. *www.thecoloradoskateboardguide.com*

Hotchkiss

North Fork Swimming Pool is located south of Hotchkiss at 333 Bulldog Lane. Open from Memorial Day through Labor Day, the pool facility includes a children's wading pool, therapy pool, and picnic area. A great way to cool off in the North Fork valley! *www.northforkrecreation.com*

Crawford

Just a stone's throw from Black Canyon of the Gunnison National Park, **Crawford State Park** provides a stunningly beautiful environment. Anglers, boaters, hikers, and water sports enthusiasts all frequent this park on the western slope. At peak times such as summer weekends, jet skiing, motor boating, and water skiing are quite popular. During the week and colder months, visitors enjoy a much more serene environment. Day-use areas include several picnic sites and a group picnicking facility near the swim beach. The Colorado Division of Parks and Wildlife, in cooperation with the U.S. Bureau of Reclamation, recently refurbished and added modern campground amenities to the park. You'll find it one mile south of Crawford along the West Elk Loop Scenic Byway: *www.byways.org* and *www.parks.state.co.us*

Paonia

The small **Paonia River Park** offers a good put-in for boating on the North Fork of the Gunnison River. Take the main Paonia Exit east from Highway 133, and look for the parking area on the left just after you cross the river.

Crawford State Park

Paonia River Park

Southern Colorado

FREMONT

CUSTER

HUERFANO

COSTILLA

ALAMOSA

SAGUACHE

RIO GRANDE

CONEJOS

Arkansas R.

Rio Grande

115

67

165

96

9

69

50

285

17

114

112

160

15

371

142

159

159

150

160

69

69

10

25

12

9

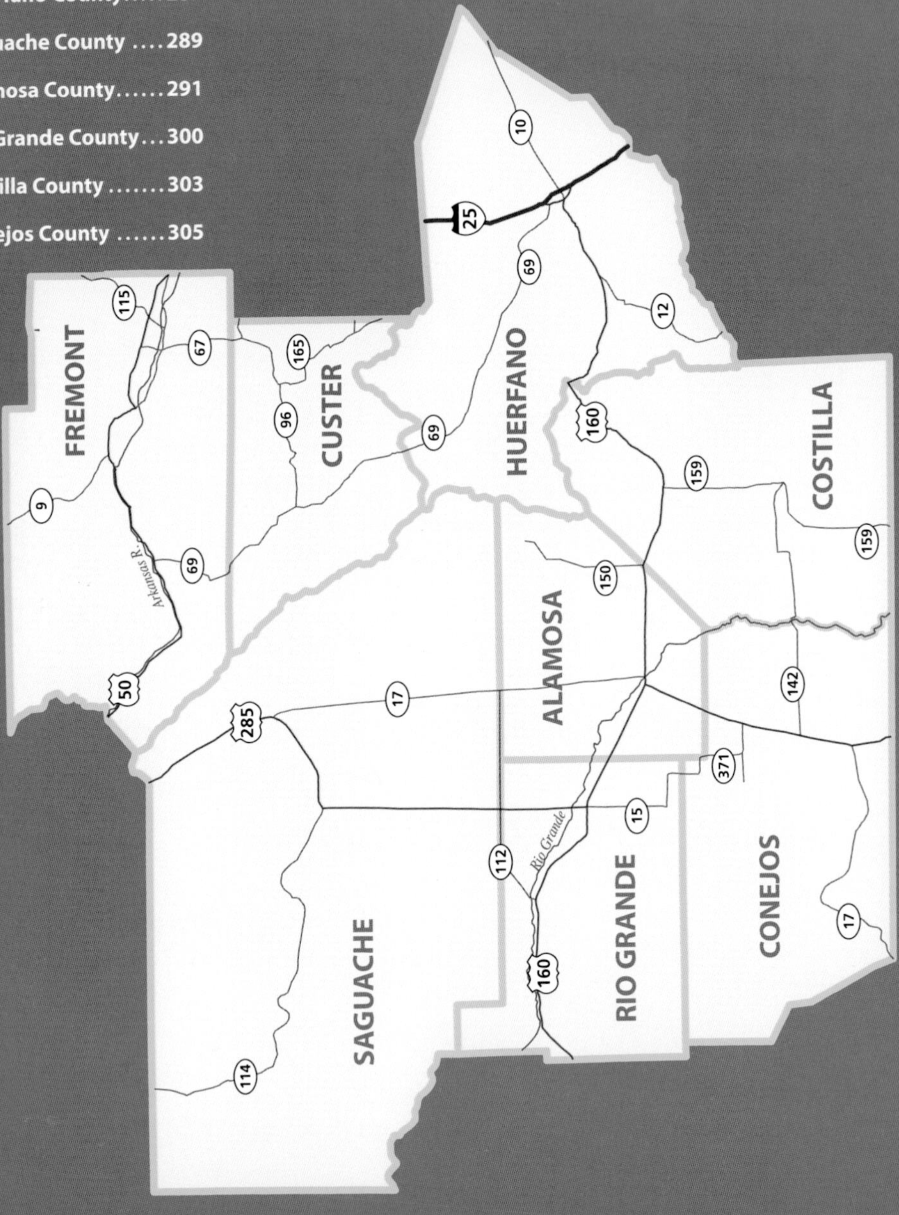

Fremont County
Florence

The 180-acre **Pathfinder Regional Park** is named for Fremont County's namesake, John C. Fremont, who earned the nickname "Pathfinder" due to his explorations between 1838 and 1854, which included mapping the West. The park includes two multi-use fields, playgrounds, picnic shelters, restroom/concession buildings, and natural areas in the open space. Eventually, the Arkansas Riverwalk will extend east from MacKenzie Avenue into the park. Plans also call for the development of a fishing area and river access trails. The excellent playground equipment features slides, games, poles, swings, and a climbing wall. The park is located between Cañon City and Florence. Head east from Cañon City on Highway 50. At the Home Depot, turn south on McKenzie Avenue, and travel 2.3 miles to Highway 115. Go east 1.8 miles to the park on the north side. *http://ccrec.tripod.com*

Pioneer Park is a small park with big beautiful trees at 3rd Street and Pikes Peak Avenue/Highway 67 in Florence.

Cañon City

Following the Arkansas River for more than seven miles, the **Arkansas Riverwalk Trail** winds its way through wetlands, cottonwoods groves, and the John Griffin Regional Park, a natural area known for its wetlands and wildlife. The hard-packed crushed-gravel surface is excellent for running, hiking, biking, and horseback riding. An early-evening stroll offers bird-watching and wildlife-viewing opportunities. Dogs are welcome, but must be leashed. To reach the parking area and trailhead, take South 9th

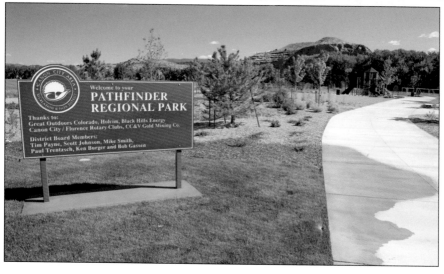

Street/Highway 115 south from Cañon City across the Arkansas River, and make the first left on Sell Street. *http://ccrec.tripod.com*

Cañon City's Whitewater Kayak and Recreation Park is a terrific addition to the town, both recreationally and aesthetically. Located between the train depot and Centennial Park, near the 4th Street viaduct, the water park's two features—Flytrap and Nessman—attract kayakers, rafters, boogie boarders, and the occasional tuber. Waves and flows vary, and both features contain washouts downstream. A wading area upstream from the Centennial Park walking bridge is great for the younger crowd. The Royal Gorge Whitewater Festival, held at the park in June, hosts a kayak throwdown, raft rodeo, kayak and raft races, and other events. Spectators can take a seat on one of the sandstone slabs that serve as bleachers on the riverbank. From Royal Gorge Boulevard/Highway 50, take 3rd Street south to the river and parking. *www.canoncity.org*

Custer County
Silver Cliff

The eight-acre **Silver Cliff Town Park** is a large part of this small 19th-century silver-mining community. An 1880 census listed the town's population as 5,040, placing Silver Cliff as the state's third largest city, behind only Denver and Leadville. Today the population is 589. Park views of the Sangre de Cristo and Wet Mountain Ranges are sublime. Facilities include a baseball field with brick dugouts, basketball court, volleyball court, skate park, picnic pavilion, as well as horseshoe pits, playground equipment, and restrooms. Find the park at South 4th Street and Lincoln Avenue on the south side of town. *www.silvercliffco.com*

Huerfano County

Lathrop State Park holds the distinction of being Colorado's first state park. Its 1,594 acres of recreational opportunities are nestled in the shadow of Southern Colorado's Spanish Peaks, which dominate the landscape. Reflection photos at sunrise are intense! Boaters, anglers, and others visit the park's two lakes for a variety of water-related activities. A warm-water lake, Martin Lake draws swimmers, water skiers, and power and sail boaters. Horseshoe Lake is a peaceful haven for canoeists, kayakers, sailors, and other wakeless boaters. Catfish, bass, walleye, trout, and blue gill thrive in both lakes, while Horseshoe Lake is known for its large tiger muskies. A pinyon-juniper woodland, diverse wetlands, and riparian and aquatic plant communities await the nature enthusiast at Lathrop. Birders watch the many migratory and resident birds, including several species of raptors, pinyon and scrub jays, western meadowlarks, and a variety of waterfowl and shorebirds that are attracted to the lakes and wetland habitats. Osprey can commonly be seen in summer, and bald eagles have become familiar winter residents. Many visitors have reported seeing roadrunners in the campground. The park is three miles west of Walsenburg on U.S. Highway 160. *www.parks.state.co.us*

Walsenburg

While you're driving into Spanish Peaks country, why not cool off in the amazing **Walsenburg Water Park**? The park boasts a lazy river, three different pools, two giant water slides, and interactive water features such as

Lathrop State Park

fountains, sprays, and dumping buckets. Both slides offer a twisting, turning ride with an invigorating splash at the end. Divers will want to check out the diving board and 12-foot deep diving well. Younger water lovers can play in the zero-entry pool without worrying that the water may be too deep. When the whistle blows, hit the deck and enjoy some refreshments from the concession stand while warming in Colorado's summer sun. The water park is at City Park on West 7th/Highway 160 at Ysidro Avenue. *www.cityofwalsenburg.com*

Saguache County

The 4,000-acre **Mishak Lakes Preserve,** owned and managed by The Nature Conservancy, is one of the largest flourishing wetland complexes in Colorado. Dozens of shallow ponds dot the landscape, making Mishak one of the state's most significant breeding and migratory habitats for wetland birds. Among those thriving here are the greater sandhill crane, white-faced ibis, Wilson's phalarope, and waterfowl and shorebirds, including the American avocet. The preserve also hosts several globally rare plants and insects, including the slender spiderflower and a butterfly that feeds on it—the San Luis Valley sand hills skipper, known to reside in Colorado only in this very valley. Also specific to the valley are two mammal subspecies, the least chipmunk and Ord's kangaroo rat. The health of this wetland system depends on a complex relationship between precipitation and ground and surface water. As the ponds dry out by midsummer, late-season rain fills them up again in August. Although water levels might fluctuate dramatically from year to year, resident plants and animals are well adapted to these cycles. For further information, including opportunities to participate in guided outings, visit *www.nature.org.*

Saguache

The northern gateway to the San Luis Valley, Saguache sits at an elevation of 7,800 feet and is surrounded by the Sangre de Cristo Mountains on the east and the San Juan Mountains on the west. Saguache, a Ute Indian name pronounced Sa-watch, translates to "Water at the Blue Earth." A trailblazer by the name of Otto Mears settled the town

Otto Mears Park

in 1867. Although his fortune began when he built his first toll road above Poncha Pass, Mears is credited with building the road now known as the famous "Million Dollar Highway" (Highway 550). **Otto Mears Park** in Saguache makes a great picnic spot while exploring the valley and surrounding mountains. It's on Highway 285 between Christy and Pitkin Avenues. While you're in town, check out the nearby Saguache County Museum, featuring seven rooms of historic displays and a 1908 jail that was used for 50 years. Alferd Packer, known as "The Maneater," was surely the jail's most notorious inmate. *www.saguache.org*

The 7,100-acre **Cochetopa State Wildlife Area** attracts hunters, fishing enthusiasts, and wildlife watchers. Cochetopa Creek runs north through the property and adjacent to Los Pinos Creek on the area's north end. Dome Reservoir, located in the bordering Dome Lakes State Wildlife Area, flows into Cochetopa Creek. The coldwater streams provide excellent fishing opportunities—mostly trout—as well as habitat for a variety of waterfowl. Dusky grouse is also hunted here. Camping and dogs are prohibited. From Gunnison, go eight miles east on Highway 50 to Highway 114. Go south 20 miles to Cochetopa Creek. *www.wildlife.state.co.us*

Cochetopa State Wildlife Area

Alamosa County
Great Sand Dunes National Park and Preserve

The official designation in 2004 of **Great Sand Dunes National Park** expanded the boundaries of a small national monument into a park and preserve of more than 150,000 acres. From a distance, the massive dunes—the tallest in North America—appear to be foothills against the backdrop of the Sangre de Cristo Mountains. The story of how the sand dunes formed is ever-evolving, but the process is thought to have begun an estimated 400,000 years ago when most of the San Luis Valley lay under a lake. The

lake eventually receded, leaving behind sand and smaller lakes (some of which exist today). The sand blew with the predominant southwesterly winds, accumulating in a natural low curve or pocket below the Sangre de Cristos. Opposing wind directions—from the valley floor toward the mountains and back—caused the dunes to grow vertically.

Human beings have known about, visited, or lived near the Great Sand Dunes for more than 11,000 years. Some of the first people to enter the San Luis Valley and the dunes area were nomadic hunters and gatherers who came to hunt the herds of mammoths and prehistoric bison that grazed nearby. These Stone Age people hunted with large stone spears or dart points now identified as Clovis and Folsom points. It is thought that they spent time here when hunting and plant gathering was good, and avoided the region during times of drought and scarcity.

Grasslands, shrublands, and wetlands surround the main dunefield on three sides, comprising more than half of the expanded national park. Geologically, these lands are critical to the sand system, but are seldom visited, creating outstanding opportunities for solitude, wildlife watching, and enjoying the open space. Abundant wildlife species inhabit the park; mule deer, in particular, are frequently spotted.

The dunefield and much of the surrounding mountains are federally-designated wilderness, making the Great Sand Dunes a unique place to explore the natural environment. Depending on snowpack, Medano Creek flows along the base of the Great Sand Dunes. It's one of the few places in the world to experience "surge flow," a phenomenon that occurs when sand falls into the creek, creating water surges and rhythmic waves. Park visitors can wade in Medano Creek, play in the sand, and hike the dunes and nearby trails heading into the backcountry. Some even sandboard, sled, or ski the dunes. Also popular is a night walk to view the spectacular light pollution-free night sky. The

Great Sand Dunes National Park and Preserve

well-maintained Pinyon Flats Campground offers both reservable and first-come, first-served sites. Backpacking in the park's back-country and primitive camping along Medano Pass Road are also permitted. *www.nps.gov*

The historic **Medano/Zapata Ranch,** which lies within Great Sand Dunes National Park boundaries, is a 103,000-acre bison and guest ranch that is home to thousands of elk, deer, coyotes, birds, and other species. About 2,500 bison roam these grasslands as part of the natural grazing ecology. Unlike typical vacations, guests of Zapata Ranch come for hands-on learning about ranching, horsemanship, and/or conservation practices. A typical day might be spent on horseback, moving/working bison, learning horse handling and riding skills, and also riding to enjoy the scenery. Guests who choose the conservation/nature option participate in interpretive hikes, photography, bird and other wildlife watching, and education on the geology and

ecology of the San Luis Valley. Public programs include bison tours and educational seminars. Public access to the ranch is available via a mile-long hiking trail through cotton-wood groves and wetlands, offering extraordinary mountain views and plentiful wildlife viewing. The trail is open March through October, from dawn to dusk. Visit *www.zranch.org* for information.

Great Sand Dunes National Park, located 35 miles northeast of Alamosa, can be reached by Highway 160 and Highway 150 from the south, or from Highway 17 and County Lane 6 from the west. To visit Zapata Ranch, drive north on Highway 150 towards the park. Just past mile marker 12, look for the ranch on the left, surrounded by a large grove of cottonwood trees. *www.nps.gov*

In the heat of summer, when the sand dunes are especially hot, visitors often head to beautiful **Zapata Falls,** just a short hike south of the park. The falls rush through a

narrow rock crevasse, originating from South Zapata Creek. The rushing water is cold and the rocks can be slippery, so wear sturdy shoes with good traction , as well as a jacket, even in summer. Since you are well above the San Luis Valley floor, looking over the sand dunes, the views are excellent. In winter, the falls and stream are frozen, and the access road may be closed. To reach Zapata Falls from the national park, take Highway 150 south for about eight miles. Look for the Zapata Falls Recreation Area sign between mile markers 10 and 11. Turn east, and drive about 3.5 miles to the trailhead. You'll find a parking lot, picnic area, restroom, and exhibits. The uphill trail to the falls is about half a mile in length. *www.nps.gov*

The 2,054-acre **San Luis State Park and Wildlife Area** lies in the shadow of Great Sand Dunes National Park. I've made some amazing reflection photographs over the years of Blanca Peak and the Sangre de Cristo Mountains from San Luis Lake. Waterfowl, shorebirds, songbirds, and raptors fill the sky over this unique desert ecosystem, making San Luis an outstanding area for wildlife watching. All 51 sites at the park's modern camping. All 51 sites at the park's modern camp-

ground have electrical hookups, sheltered tables, fire grills, nearby drinking water hydrants, and an available dump station, as well as a panoramic view of San Luis Lake, the surrounding Sangre de Cristo Mountain Range, and the Great Sand Dunes. Since the 1920s, San Luis has been considered a water sports haven in the San Luis Valley. Enthusiasts come to water ski, motorboat, jet ski, fish, sail, and windsurf. Four miles of wide, level gravel trails in the wildlife area provide an easy hike or mountain bike ride through the low dunes and wetlands. These hard-surfaced gravel trails are also ADA-accessible. Sandy trails allow limited access into the dunes and wetlands areas.

The park's variety of natural environments—wetlands, lakes, and the dry valley floor—provide excellent habitat for a variety of wildlife, and outstanding viewing opportunities. The calm waters attract migratory waterfowl and other birds, and coyotes, kangaroo rats, and rabbits are commonly seen in the surrounding dunes. Elk, songbirds, raptors, reptiles, and amphibians find refuge in an unusual riparian oasis hidden in the low dunes. These protected lands also preserve crucial habitat for rare flora and fauna.

San Luis State Park and Wildlife Area

This lovely park is located just 15 minutes west of the Great Sand Dunes. Take Highway 160 west from Alamosa, and turn north on Highway 150 (the turnoff for the dunes). Travel 13.5 miles and turn west on Six Mile Lane. Continue for eight miles and then turn north one-eighth mile to the park. *www.parks.state.co.us*

Higel State Wildlife Area is named for the Higel family, who have owned and operated Higel Ranch, on the Rio Grande River since the early 1900s. When the Higels sold half of their riparian corridor land and substantial water rights to the Colorado Division of Wildlife in 1997 (now the Division of Parks and Wildlife), the state wildlife area was created. By protecting their land permanently through a conservation easement, the Higels are able to continue their tradition of cattle grazing and haying, and also ensure the sustainability of habitat for wildlife, including the federally-endangered southwestern willow flycatcher. The 1,129-acre property offers fishing, wildlife watching, and hunting for deer, dove, waterfowl, turkey, and small game. From Alamosa, drive approximately 9.5 miles northwest on Highway 160, turn east on County Road 3 South, and drive three miles. Turn north at the sign onto the access road to reach the parking area. *www.wildlife.state.co.us*

Alamosa
Meaning "cottonwood" in Spanish, Alamosa was incorporated in August, 1878. It's the hub of the San Luis Valley and home to Adams State College. *www.cityofalamosa.org*

Sunrise Park offers spectacular views of Blanca Peak to the west. Go north on Highway 17 on the east side of town to McKinney Avenue. Head east to the park at Haniver Street. A bit bigger than Sunrise, **Cole Park** boasts some nice shade trees. Take State Avenue north from Highway 160/6th Street to 2nd Street. Make a right to the park. **Friends Park** can

Sunrise Park

Cole Park

be found by taking Highway 285 south from Highway 160 to 8th Street. Go east to Railroad Avenue, and south to the park on the right.

The **John W. Mumma Native Aquatic Species Restoration Facility** provides shelter and care for the brood stock of Colorado's threatened and endangered native fish, plus one unique toad species that dwells in the state's highest elevations. These fish "are key to preserving the wildlife heritage of Colorado's

Higel State Wildlife Area

streams and rivers, and to preserving the state's power of self-determination in management of its waters and waterways." A large collection of tanks, ponds, and aquaria at the facility provide temporary homes to 13 native species— 12 fish and the boreal toad—with the goal of raising healthy populations that can be released back into the wild. When you visit,

stop at the adjacent Playa Blanca State Wildlife Area for wildlife watching opportunities. Only group tours are allowed, so call ahead at 719-587-3392. Free pamphlets and brochures are available. The restoration facility and lake are located west of Alamosa and one mile south of Highway 160/285 on County Road 106. *www.wildlife.state.co.us*

Rio Grande County

In 1953, the Migratory Bird Conservation Commission established the **Monte Vista National Wildlife Refuge** to provide a much-needed habitat for wildlife—particularly waterfowl—in the San Luis Valley. Numerous dikes and other water control structures feed a patchwork of diverse wetland habitats ranging from shallow wet meadows to open water. Water is supplied by artesian wells, pumped wells, and irrigation canals—some dating back to the "ditch boom" of the 1880s. Other management tools include

mowing, grazing, prescribed burning, and farming—all critical to ensuring that refuge lands continue to provide food, cover, and nesting habitat for waterfowl and other water birds.

The refuge is a major stopover for migrating greater sandhill cranes traveling between their winter home around New Mexico's Bosque del Apache National Wildlife Refuge and breeding grounds in the northern U.S. and southern Canada. Up to 20,000 cranes pass through in the spring and again in the fall. Three endangered whooping cranes—

all that remain from a failed attempt to establish a wild migratory population in the 1980s—can be seen migrating with the sandhill crane. In the 1980s, a single herd of elk began using the refuge. Now, several hundred come for winter food and to escape hunting threats on nearby public lands. The refuge can be viewed along a four-mile auto tour, as well as from county roads open year round. Drive eight miles south from Monte Vista on Highway 15 to reach the visitor's center. *www.fws.gov*

Monte Vista

During the summer of 1881, when the railroad was extended from Alamosa to Del Norte, a watering tank was established on a plot of land known as the Lariat siding. It was here that Lillian Fassett opened the first store in what was to become Monte Vista. The next year, the original townsite was platted and called Lariat. On May 1, 1884, the town was renamed Henry in honor of its promoter, T.C. Henry. Two years later, in 1886, the town was incorporated and renamed Monte Vista (Spanish for "mountain view"). *www.monte-vista.org*

Slightly more than seven acres, **Chapman Park** is Monte Vista's largest park. It features

Natural Wonders of the San Luis Valley Play Park

a playground, sand volleyball court, and pavilion with grills and picnic tables. The .58-mile walking/jogging path loops around the park, which offers plenty of space for playing football, soccer, and other activities. The park is on the west side of town, just north of Highway 160/285 at Chico Camino Street.

Next to Marsh Elementary School, **Natural Wonders of the San Luis Valley Play Park** contains a playground uniquely designed with the nature of the valley in mind. Go north on Lyell Street from Highway 160/285 to the park on your left. *www.cityofmontevista.com*

Rio Grande State Wildlife Area highlights hunting, fishing, hiking, and wildlife viewing. Along the Rio Grande, bald eagles sometimes roost above the river. The nearby wetlands south of the river host great blue heron and common waterfowl. The cottonwoods lining the water's edge peak in their fall color around the second week in October, making beautiful photographs. Drive north two miles from Highway 160 on County Line Road (Rio Grande County Road 6E/Alamosa County Road S-100) between Monte Vista and Alamosa.

Approximately 324 acres, **Home Lake State Wildlife Area** borders Rio Grande State Wild-life Area, offering abundant fishing opportunities. Rainbow trout, northern pike, and channel catfish are caught at Home Lake, which also offers great scenery and waterfowl observations. From Monte Vista, go 1.5 miles east on Sherman Avenue. *www.wildlife.state.co.us*

Chapman Park

Rio Grande State Wildlife Area

Home Lake State Wildlife Area

Del Norte

By the mid-1870s, prospectors discovered that the nearby San Juan Mountains were rich in gold and silver deposits. Many mining claims were registered, and the mining furor began. The scenic Del Norte region had attracted people before, however, when Spaniards visited the area in 1859. Whether it was the gold or the area's location of "Gateway to the San Juans," Del Norte's occupants stuck around and incorporated the town in 1872.

Located 15 miles east of South Fork, Del Norte and the backdrop of the San Juans make a spectacular location for a skate park. Bring the kids along and visit the **Del Norte Skate Park,** located in the north part of town. From Highway 160, go north on Columbia Avenue, and then west on 2nd Street. The skate park will be on your right.

Costilla County
Fort Garland

With views of Mount Blanca, Colorado's fourth highest peak, **Town Park** is a great place to stop while touring the San Luis Valley. It's located one block north of Highway 160 on Beaubien Avenue on the left.

San Luis

Founded in 1851, San Luis is Colorado's oldest town that was part of a Mexican land grant. An extremely rich Hispanic culture—including the language, religion, and way of life—has been passed on for generations. A meadowland called **La Vega** provides communal grazing for cattle, as well as close access to mountain terrain where residents can

hunt, recreate, and gather timber. Only two commons exist in the United States—Boston Commons and the Vega Commons—and only Vega retains its original usage, which is communal grazing. Between May and October, visitors will find local residents outside watching their cattle. To view La Vega, look for the stone commemorative marker at the south edge of town on the west side of CO Hwy 159 (Main Street) in San Luis. It is best to call ahead before exploring La Vega since the lands are not open to the general public.

The southern Sangre de Cristo landscape, comprised primarily of old Spanish land grants, contains some of the state's largest remaining private ownerships. Until recently, the areas surrounding the Southern Sangre de Cristo Mountains—the Spanish Peaks on the east and the San Luis Valley on the west—have remained largely secluded agricultural communities.

Covering parts of Conejos, Costilla, and Alamosa Counties, the **Sangre de Cristo National Heritage Area** recognizes this area as the confluence of American Indian, Latino, and Anglo cultures. The National Heritage Area program is administered by the National Park Service to highlight distinctive landscapes shaped by natural, historic, and recreational resources. Nine potential conservation areas within this setting have been identified to contain species found almost nowhere else on earth. *www.coloradoopenlands.org*

La Vega

Conejos County
Antonito

Antonito serves as the eastern terminus of the Cumbres & Toltec Narrow Gauge Railroad, one of the few surviving 19th century Colorado railroads. If you haven't already, take the train ride to Chama, New Mexico. It is a "must do" when in Colorado. From Highway 285, **Town Park** is found by going west on West 6th Avenue to Aspen Street.

Southwest Colorado

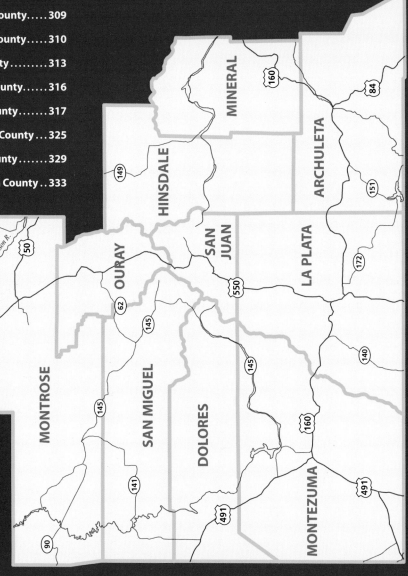

Hinsdale County
Lake City

Lake Fork Memorial Park is a fine place for a picnic when you're visiting this quaint town, deep in the heart of Colorado's San Juan Mountains. With a dog park, skate park, softball diamond, accessible fishing pier, soccer fields, and restrooms, the park is located at the confluence of Henson Creek and the Lake Fork of the Gunnison River. Take 7th Street east from Highway 149 to the park on Henson Street. *www.lakecity.com*

Lake City's namesake, **Lake San Cristobal,** was formed hundreds of years ago by a rare natural earth flow called the Slumgullion slide, which blocked the Lake Fork of the Gunnison River. Lake San Cristobal is the second-largest natural lake in Colorado, and a variety of trout live in its cold waters. Visitors can fish from any public access area along the shore, including those near the lake outlet and those located on the east side of the lake along County Road 33 at Wupperman Campground. Or, you can float your boat and fish from the surface. State catch and possession limits apply, and licenses are required. From Lake City, travel south on Highway 149 for two miles. Then, take a right onto County Road 30, and go 1.5 miles to the junction of County Road 33. Turn left, and travel two miles (the road becomes gravel). You'll notice Wupperman Campground on the right.

Like most water sources, Lake San Cristobal attracts a wide variety of wildlife, especially during warmer seasons. Canada geese can usually be seen at the lake outlet near the junction of County Roads 30 and 33. Migratory birds, including geese and a variety of ducks, are viewed at the marshy, south end of the lake, along with smaller birds and beavers. If you're lucky, you might spot an elk or a moose.

The picturesque Red Mountain Gulch Day Use Area lies close to the marshy end of the lake where many birds and other wildlife can be seen. It's a great location for a small picnic or a large gathering. Facilities include several picnic sites, each with a picnic table and grill, plus a pavilion shelter with a large outdoor cooking grill. Restrooms are available seasonally. Located at the south end of Lake San Cristobal on County Road 30, the Day Use Area offers parking, as does the area by the bridge at the lake inlet a little further up the road. *www.lakecity.com*

Mineral County
Creede

Creede Skate Park is somewhat of an anomaly in this historic mining town, which dates back to the 19th century. The park is surrounded by relics of the past! You'll see it on the right as you're heading out of town on Highway 149 toward Lake City. *www.creede.com*

Lake San Cristobal

Archuleta County
Pagosa Springs

The expansive **Pagosa Springs Sports Complex** lies along the beautiful banks of the San Juan River. It has athletic fields, and paved hiking and biking trails. Take Hot Springs Boulevard south from Highway 160/Main Street to Apache Street. Go west to 5th Street and south to the park. *www.townofpagosasprings.com*

Navajo State Park is Colorado's answer to Lake Powell. Extending 20 miles south into New Mexico, Navajo Reservoir attracts campers and boaters year-round. House-boaters and other power-boaters especially love cruising the 15,000 surface-acres of this giant reservoir. Boaters can gas up at the park's Two Rivers Marina, which also offers daily and seasonal slip and mooring ball rentals. All 138 campsites in Navajo's camp-grounds are open every day of the year.

Anglers take to the water to catch crap-pie, large-mouth and small-mouth bass, northern pike, trout, bluegill, and catfish. Wildlife watching is another popular activity here, and winter is the perfect time of year to do it. Typically arriving early in December to winter in Arboles, bald eagles perch in trees overlooking the lake where they can hunt for prey and bask in the sun. Deer wander the campgrounds, and frequent the visitor center and picnic grounds, looking for grass, berries, and other edible items. Canadian geese camp out for the winter near the lake and in the fields, or stop by on their way to warmer winter climates. Take Highway 160 west from Pagosa Springs for 17 miles. Then turn south onto Highway 151 for 18 miles to Arboles. Turn left again onto County Road 982, and drive two miles to the park. *www.parks.state.co.us*

Cerise Regional Park

Montrose County
Montrose

Cerise Regional Park has more than 110 acres of outdoor amenities and lies within the larger **Clifford E. Baldridge Regional Park.** Amenities at Cerise include a multi-purpose field, playground, pond, bike path, picnic tables and shelter, and access to the scenic Uncompahgre River. It's a great place to beat the heat! To get there, go west on Main Street across the Uncompahgre River to Chipeta Road, and then south to the park on the left. **Montrose Skate Park** lies within the main

Chief Ouray Memorial Park

portion of Baldridge Park. From Highway 550, go west on South 5th Street to South Rio Grande Avenue. Go south to Apollo Road, west to Colorado Avenue, and south to the park, which also lies along the Uncompahgre River. *www.cityofmontrose.org*

Chief Ouray Memorial Park and the Ute Indian Museum lie in the heart of traditional Ute territory on the original 8.65-acre homestead owned by Chief Ouray and his wife, Chipeta. Built in 1956 and expanded in 1998, the museum offers one of the most complete collections of the Ute people. In addition to the Chief Ouray Memorial Park, the grounds include Chipeta's crypt and a native plants garden. The museum also includes the Montrose Visitor Information Center, gallery space, classrooms, and a store. Take Highway 550 to the south end of Montrose. After crossing the Uncompahgre River, take the first right on Chipeta Road. The park is immediately on your left. *www.historycolorado.org*

Olathe

A fun, family event featuring all the free "Olathe Sweet" sweet corn you can eat occurs

Olathe Community Park

annually each August. It began back in 1992 when a few Olathe residents decided to organize a celebration of the region's primary crop, Olathe Sweet Corn. More than just the area's agricultural jewel, sweet corn is the product that kept this rural community alive at a time when other efforts failed. The **Olathe Sweet Corn Festival** became so successful over the years that the town's facilities could no longer accommodate it. A new site was found, the property was developed, and in 1996, the 37-acre, multi-use **Olathe Community Park** became the permanent home of the sweet corn festival, as well as a year-round recreational facility for residents.

"Giving the people what they want" has long been the festival staff's mantra. If you have a chance to attend, you'll see for yourself why organizers contend that the festival is, and always has been, about people. Olathe's pride and joy has brought people together for several years, providing them with a strong sense of community and accomplishment. It also has accomplished wonderful things for the community itself—socially, economically, and culturally. More than 16,000 visitors attend the Olathe Sweet Corn Festival each year, and plans are underway to make it a two-day event. *www.olathesweetcornfest.com*

Ridgway Recreation Corridor

Ouray County
Ridgway

For years now, I've been raving about Ridgway and its proximity to Dallas Divide on Highway 62. The Divide provides stunning views of the magnificent Sneffels Range, which includes the prominent 14,150-foot Mount Sneffels. Ralph Lauren's Double RL Ranch serves as Sneffel's famous foreground, and Last Dollar Road and County Roads 5, 7, and 9 are equally famous for their access to some of Colorado's most extraordinary aspen colors in the spring and fall. As a result, many folks bypass Ridgway on their way to view the scenery. (See my guidebook, *John Fielder's Best of Colorado,* for details.)

The Town of Ridgway, however, is certainly worth a stop. In addition to the quaint restaurants and accommodations, the town and its surrounding mountains and valleys have been the setting for several Hollywood western movies, including *True Grit* starring John Wayne. You'll also be impressed by the 27-acre **Ridgway Recreation Corridor,** which includes the seven-acre **Ridgway Town Park** and the paved three-mile **Uncompahgre Riverway Trail,** connecting to the Ridgway State Park and Reservoir trail system. A new pedestrian bridge across the river in Ridgway completes the loop. This portion of the river was once an industrial eyesore, but today the kokanee salmon are swimming, migratory birds are returning, and a bald eagle community winters along the river. There's much to photograph here. You'll find the peaceful and picturesque Ridgway Town Park on the northwest side of the Uncompahgre River as you enter town from Highway 550. Hang a quick right after the bridge to get to the parking area. *www.town.ridgway.co.us*

Ridgway State Park boasts stunning mountain scenery, magnificent campgrounds, modern and universally-accessible recreation areas, and a five-mile-long reservoir for boating, fishing, and swimming. The park also features picnic and playground areas, extensive trails, and diverse wildlife. Only 15 miles from the Town of Ouray—known as the "Switzerland of America"—Ridgway is popular with outdoor enthusiasts year-round.

Wildlife viewing is another favorite pastime at Ridgway. Mammal species include elk, bobcat, mountain lion, coyote, yellow-bellied marmot, red fox and cottontail rabbit. Mule deer can be seen grazing through the campgrounds often throughout the year. Black bear occasionally enter the park when food sources are scarce, but primarily inhabit higher, more alpine environments. You'll find especially good habitat on the western side of the reservoir for reptile species such as sagebrush lizard, short-horned lizard, and collared lizard.

Ridgway State Park

Bring along the binoculars for the 140 species of migratory and resident birds that have been identified, including many species of waterfowl and shorebirds. Confirmed breeders in the park include the American dipper, black-chinned hummingbird, red-naped sapsucker, white-throated swift, red-tailed hawk, and many others. Northern harrier and osprey are common raptors, and Northern goshawks and American Peregrine falcons also have been observed. Bald eagles winter here from November to April, while golden eagles are year-round residents.

Anglers fish for rainbow trout, brown trout, kokanee salmon, and the occasional yellow perch on the reservoir and in-flowing streams. Crayfish are also abundant in the reservoir. Boaters can reach secluded coves on the west shore of the reservoir; Mears Bay Cove offers great shoreline fishing; and Pa-Co-Chu-Puk's two ponds are stocked with rainbow trout for three youth fishing events held during the summer months. Also in Pa-Co-Chu-Puk, a popular one-mile section of the Uncompahgre River below the dam makes for good catch-and-release fly-fishing.

From Montrose, drive Highway 550 south for 22 miles to the park entrance on the right side of the road. From Ridgway, go north on 550 for four miles to the park entrance on the left side of the road. *www.parks.state.co.us*

Encompassing 175 mountain acres and sitting at an elevation of 8,580 feet, **Top of the Pines** is a unique open space preserve that serves as an outdoor classroom and learning facility. Acquired by Ouray County as a rustic "living-classroom retreat," the preserve's mission includes preserving the land for open space and wildlife habitat. Both public and private groups and organizations are welcome to use the preserve; fees vary. The property features a spacious mountain meadow, the seasonal West Lake, and spectacular views of both the Mount Sneffels and the Cimarron Ranges. A natural amphitheater, framed by Mt. Sneffels, is accessible from the main entrance. An extensive cross-country skiing and hiking trail system weaves through the ponderosa pines and alpine meadows. For information about visiting the preserve, visit *www.topofthepines.org.*

Top of the Pines

Ouray

Ironton Historical Site preserves the 19th century mining town site and a few of its original buildings. Founded in 1883 and located at the north end of the Red Mountain Mining District, the wealthy Town of Ironton served as a transportation junction, and a stage and supply center. Sulphuric acid in the area destroyed the metal machinery used in the mines, which led to their closing. Look for Forest Service signs to the site on the east side of Highway 550, about one mile north of the last switchback descending Red Mountain Pass toward Ouray. *www.ouraycolorado.com*

San Juan County
Silverton

With eastern views of the Alps-like Needle Mountains, the 137-acre **Molas Lake Park and Campground** sits among some of the most spectacular peaks in the Rocky Mountains. The short drive to Little Molas Lake provides one of the best Colorado reflection photos I've ever seen! Tents, trailers, campers, and RVs are all welcome at Molas campground. Guests enjoy fishing the park's well-stocked, 25-acre lake, and can gain immediate access to the Colorado Trail. The park offers a plethora of hiking, biking, and mountaineering opportu-

Ironton Historical Site

Animas Mountain

nities. This is a commercial park and campground, so be prepared to pay the required fees. Campground reservations are recommended, but not required. Molas is easy to find since it's the only non-natural thing on this stretch of the Million Dollar Highway (Highway 550), seven miles south of Silverton on the east side of the road. *www.molaslake.com*

Kendall Mountain Recreation Area, a local ski hill in Silverton, features a family-friendly lift, ice skating rink, sledding hill, snowshoeing trails, cross-country and backcountry skiing, and ski and snowboard lessons. Ice skates, sleds, snowshoes, and skis can be rented on site. Take Greene Street (the main street) north through town to 14th Street, and then head west to Kendall. *www.skikendall.com*

La Plata County
Durango

Nearly 178 acres, **Dalla Mountain Park** lies adjacent to the Bureau of Land Management's **Animas Mountain** natural trail system. Together, they afford several miles of hiking and mountain biking opportunities in the foothills northwest of Durango. The spruce, fir, and ponderosa pine forest ecosystem provides habitat for elk, deer, black bear, and mountain lion. Bring along your camera in the fall for great color photos of the scrub

Molas Lake Park and Campground

Horse Gulch

oak. From downtown Durango, travel north on Main Avenue/Highway 550, and turn west onto 25th Street, which turns into Junction Street. Make a right on Birket Drive after a mile or so. The trail starts at the dead end of Birket where you'll see the Animas Mountain trailhead sign. *www.durangogov.org*

Horse Gulch consists of a 57-mile system of unpaved trails in the hilly region just beyond Fort Lewis College. This 1,295-acre park contains diverse vegetation and wildlife habitat. Easily accessible from town, Horse Gulch is a favorite hiking, biking, and jogging destination for locals and visitors—it's also where the pros ride! The scenery from the mesa is outstanding with views of the San Juan Mountains to the north and west. You'll find the trailhead on 3rd Street and 9th Avenue. From downtown Durango, travel south on Main Avenue to College Drive and turn left. At the intersection of College Drive and 8th Avenue, turn right. Go south to 3rd Street and turn left. Limited parking is available at the end of the street. *www.durangogov.org*

As part of the Animas River Greenway, the hard-surfaced **Animas River Trail** runs for seven miles through Durango along the beautiful Animas River. Hikers and bikers enjoy views of the river and its many rafters, kayakers, and tubers. This popular trail stretches from 32nd Street and E. 2nd Avenue on the north end to the south side of town, crossing 12 city parks and five bridges along the way. **Dallabetta Park,** one of these parks on the south end, is a great place for a picnic along the river. From downtown Durango, travel south on Main Avenue, and turn right onto College Drive. At the light, turn left onto Camino Del Rio. Go 3.75 miles to River Road, and turn right. Cross the bridge, take another right, and you'll see the park on your right. *www.durangogov.org*

Formerly known as Durango Mountain Park, the 301.6-acre **Overend Mountain Park** encompasses a hilly area on the west side of Durango. Just over 12 miles of natural-surface trails wind their way through the pine and shrub oak-covered terrain. Renamed in 2010 for local resident and mountain biking legend Ned Overend, the park's trails range from

Overend Mountain Park

Animas River Trail

Dallabetta Park

tame and level at the bottom, to extremely challenging on the Hogback and other steeper areas. I've seen people riding up and down theses dirt hills on inclines approaching 45 degrees. Just imagine biking down a twisting playground slide, and you get the picture! The hills are formed largely of Mancos Shale, which is known to degrade into chunky grey dirt that provides a decent grip. Particularly popular with singletrack mountain bikers, the trails are also frequented by hikers and joggers. Beware if you're walking the trails when they're wet, as the dirt transforms into slippery mud. Take Main Avenue to 9th Street, turn right on Roosa, and then left on Avendia del Sol. Park up by the Elle Vita neighborhood, and ride/hike straight ahead to the back of the area. (It's not the easiest trailhead to find.) *www.durangogov.org*

Durango Skate Park is located in beautiful Schneider Park. From Main Avenue, turn west onto 9th Street. Go past the stoplight, and turn right onto Roosa Avenue. To reach Schneider Park, make the first right turn into the parking lot. For the skate park, turn right into the second parking area. *www.durangogov.org*

Riverview Sports Complex has picnic tables, two ball fields, restrooms, and a playground, all situated on 11 acres of lovely grass. From downtown Durango, go north on Main Avenue to 15th Street and turn east. Stay left as the road merges into Florida Road. From the intersection of Florida, 15th Street, and 3rd Avenue, go approximately 1.25 miles. Turn north onto Aspen Drive, and take the first left onto Plymouth Drive. The parking lot for the complex is on the right.

At nearly 38 acres, **Chapman Hill** is a small ski area and ice rink, located right in town. Follow the directions above to Riverview Sports Complex, but after the intersection, only travel about one-half mile. You'll see Chapman Hill on the right. *www.durangogov.org*

Bayfield

Featuring several lovely shade trees, **Town Park** is a fine location for a picnic when traveling to or from Durango. Go south from Highway 160 on 160 Business to the park at West Mill Street.

Riverview Sports Complex

Ignacio

Ignacio is located on the Southern Ute Indian Reservation. The town's **Shoshone Park** has a basketball court, picnic area, nature trail, and tennis courts. You'll find it at Browning Avenue and Lampert Street.

San Miguel County
Telluride

The 12.6-mile **Galloping Goose Trail** provides abundant views of snowy mountaintops and forested hillsides, as well as occasional wildlife sightings. Don't forget your camera! With access just four miles southwest of Telluride, this popular and historic trail is also one of Colorado's most scenic, offering some of the best mountain vistas anywhere in North America. The views remind me of those in Montana's Glacier National Park.

Users travel over two trail bridges, past a restored train trestle, through a highway underpass, along segments of the historic Rio Grande Southern railway, and through the deep gullies of Uncompahgre National Forest. The diverse route, which is maintained by the U.S. Forest Service, travels along forest roads, singletrack trail, and portions of the railroad grade. Galloping Goose Trail is also known as the season's first and last skiable trail, consistently receiving more snow than any other Nordic trail in the area. Prime ski and snowshoe time generally falls

San Miguel County

between the months of October and April, with the rest of the year devoted to hikers and bikers. Watch for interesting historical landmarks along the way.

Due to its gradually increasing elevation, Galloping Goose is rated an intermediate-level trail. If you're looking for less of a challenge, start at Lawson Hill (near the intersection of Highway 145 and the 145 spur into Telluride) and ride toward South Fork Road. The most heavily-used segment of the trail, this out-and-back section also offers the most instructional signage. The trail section running from Sunshine Road to Ophir Loop is considered the most scenic. Heading south, you'll follow the San Miguel River, passing several old railroad ties—reminders of the trail's historical significance. The river here offers amazing views at dawn and dusk. From Ophir Loop, travel to the trail's southern terminus at Lizard Head Pass. This heavily-forested five-mile segment hugs Trout Lake, and is maintained in the winter by the Telluride Nordic Association. This portion also passes the last historical trestle along the route. *www.railstotrails.org* and *www.fs.usda.gov*. From Telluride, travel west on Highway 145 for approximately three miles, and turn south at the highway intersection. Proceed about one-third of a mile, turning right at the gas station onto the Lawson Hill access road. Continue for about one-half mile, following Galloping Goose Detour signs to the trailhead. (If you'd like to add a bit more mileage, take the paved bike trail all the way from town and go through the Lawson Hill Underpass tunnel.)*

The **Telluride Skate Park** is about as scenic as they get! Once in town, travel all the way to the end of Colorado Avenue. Park in the lot at **Telluride Town Park** on the south side of the street. The skate park is just past the stage area on the west side of the baseball field. The center of many activities, including the renowned Telluride Blue Grass Festival held each June, the expansive Town

Park has a campground, softball and soccer fields, basketball courts, kids' fishing pond, and many other recreational facilities. **Telluride River Park** features a delightful trail along the San Miguel River in downtown Telluride. One stretch, containing lovely wetlands, runs between the dead ends of Fir and Pine Streets south of downtown. *www.telluride-co.gov*

In 1995, the San Miguel Conservation Foundation and the Town of Telluride acquired the 320 acres adjacent to Town Park, now known as the **Bear Creek Preserve.** Expanded to include a total of 381 acres of the pristine mountain canyon, the preserve offers one of the better day hikes in Southwest Colorado. A steady 2.5-mile climb leads to upper Bear Creek Falls and connects to the Wasatch Trail and Bridal Veil Basin, offering unlimited photo opportunities. From downtown Telluride, walk to the end of Pine Street, and cross the river to the Bear Creek Trailhead.

* Text courtesy of the Rails-to-Trails Conservancy.

Telluride River Park

Bear Creek Preserve

A few minutes up the trail, check out the interesting display of interpretive maps and related information. After about two miles, you'll encounter a large boulder and just beyond that the beautiful waterfall. Views along the road-grade trail include remnants of an old wooden flume that transported water to a hydroelectric plant under the lower falls, and is said to have powered the mills in Bear Creek back in the 1890s. *www.telluride-co.gov*

Down Valley Park contains a nice playground and open space right along the scenic San Miguel River between Placerville and the Fall Creek Road. You'll see it on the south side of Highway 145. *www.sanmiguelcounty.org*

Dolores County

Encompassing 11,760 acres of incredible scenic land, **Lone Mesa State Park** lies 23 miles north of the Town of Dolores. Ranging in elevation from approximately 7,200 feet to just over 9,000 feet, the park fully encompasses the geographical feature of Lone Mesa, as well as the headwaters of Plateau Creek. Moving north through the park, the landscape transitions from open shrubland and meadow to rolling hillsides of Gambel oak intermingled with ponderosa pine. These low-density pine forests host a number of nesting and roosting sites, and provide excellent habitat for a variety of wildlife species. Visitors to these mid-level elevations often catch a glimpse of elk, deer, or black bear.

Much of what the park is famous for lies above 8,000 feet. As you climb through the canyons leading to the top of Lone Mesa, you'll pass healthy aspen trees, ponderosas more than 400-years-old, and canyon "rim zones" featuring brilliant swathes of golden aspen in the fall, as well as Douglas fir and pine forests. Although the elusive lynx is attracted to this diverse rim habitat, its visits are thought to be short-term. Bobcats, however, are often spotted along the climb to the mesa. Once on top, you're rewarded with breathtaking views of the La Plata Mountains, Lone Cone, and the 14,000-foot peaks surrounding Telluride. Take some time to enjoy the vantage point, as well as the surrounding geology. If you catch yourself on the mesa at nighttime, be sure to gaze into the expanse of stars in the light pollution-free sky above you.

Lone Mesa State Park

Rico Town Park

Mancos State Park

As of the publication of this guide, the park is closed to most public access while development and management planning occurs. However, a limited number of folks accessing the park under its high-quality public hunting program and through volunteer park stewardship projects are getting a sneak peak at Lone Mesa's splendor. Contact the Colorado Division of Parks and Wildlife for updates on access. *www.parks.state.co.us*

Rico

Much remains of Rico's 19th century mining days, and the town is now a bedroom community to Telluride. Rico lies in the very scenic East Fork of the Dolores River valley where autumn colors are extraordinary. **Rico Town Park** sits behind the school on Commercial Street, one block east of Highway 145.

Montezuma County
Dolores

The 15,000-square-foot **Ron Kotarski Memorial Playground** was built in five days by hundreds of volunteers. The playground provides a great place to stop with the kids when traveling in Dolores River country north of Cortez, or driving the back way to Telluride. It's on the west end of town at 101 Railroad Avenue.

Mancos

A haven for the year-round outdoor enthusiast, **Mancos State Park** and its Jackson Gulch Reservoir offer endless hours of enjoyment in the spring, summer, and fall for canoeists, kayakers, and wakeless power-boaters. Depending on conditions, winter provides great opportunities for cross-country skiing, snowshoeing, and ice fishing. Anglers here catch numerous species of fish, including yellow perch and rainbow trout. The park's two campgrounds are used by travelers from across the state and country when visiting the area's attractions, which include Durango, Mesa Verde National Park, the San Juan Skyway, and the San Juan National Forest,

Boyle Park

which features hundreds of miles of snowmobile trails. The West Mancos Trailhead is just two miles from Mancos State Park. To get there, turn north on Highway 184 from Highway 160 at the Town of Mancos. *www.parks.state.co.us*

Boyle Park is right behind the longstanding Cox Conoco Station on East Grand Avenue south of Highway 160.

Cortez

Although Cortez is best known for its proximity to Mesa Verde National Park, the town offers its own collection of parks to enjoy when visitors aren't exploring ancient cliff dwellings. Given that Colorado's Four Corners region gets plenty hot in summer, the **Cortez Municipal Aquatics Complex** makes for a cool destination. Open seven days a week, locals and visitors alike can splash around in the outdoor pool from Memorial Day weekend through Labor Day weekend. Both kids and adults love the complex's 125-foot, double-loop water slide, diving board, tube slides, splash pad, and a regulated-depth baby pool. Locker rooms are equipped with showers and lockers. Outside food or coolers are not allowed, as concessions are sold on site. You'll find the aquatics complex on the northwest cor-

ner of **Cortez City Park** at Montezuma Avenue and Park Street, one block north of Highway 160/Main Street.

Parque de Vida

Parque de Vida and **Centennial Park** complete the downtown Cortez park system, boasting open space, trails, wetlands, ball fields, and a skate park. Separated by North Mildred Road, the two parks are located north of E. Montezuma Avenue across from City Park. *www.cityofcortez.com*

When you visit **Lewis Arriola Park** north of Cortez, you'll walk in the tracks Anasazi Indians made 1,000 years ago. The park offers an historic stopover with modern amenities, including a ball field, volleyball court, picnic area, and walking trails. From Cortez, drive 10 miles north on Highway 491 to County Road South. Go west one mile to the park.

Index

John Fielder

John Fielder has worked tirelessly to promote the protection of Colorado's ranches, open spaces, and wildlands during his 30-year career as a nature photographer. His photography has influenced people and legislation, earning him recognition including the Sierra Club's Ansel Adams Award in 1993 and, in 2011, the Aldo Leopold Foundation's first Achievement Award given to an individual.

He was a member of the 1990 committee appointed by Governor Roy Romer to explore ways in which to invest in protecting and enhancing Colorado's outdoor heritage, as well as a member of the citizen's committee that placed the Great Outdoors Colorado (GOCO) initiative on the 1992 ballot. He traveled the state that year to share his photographs of Colorado with interested people and organizations, and to speak on behalf of the measure that dedicates virtually all Colorado Lottery proceeds to recreation, open space and wildlife. In 1993, he was appointed by Governor Romer to the Great Outdoors Colorado Board, and served two four-year terms.

John approached the Great Outdoors Colorado Board in 2010 and beseeched it to consider celebrating GOCO's 20th anniversary in 2012 with the publication of this guide book, *Guide to Colorado's Great Outdoors: Lottery-Funded Parks, Trails, Wildlife Areas & Open Spaces,* and a picture book, *Colorado's Great Outdoors: Celebrating 20 Years of Lottery-Funded Lands,* depicting many of the places invested in by GOCO. The board partnered with him to photograph hundreds of county and city open spaces, wildlife habitat, state parks and wildlife areas, local and regional trails, and community parks, ball fields, and playgrounds. John drove 35,000 miles in less than two years from one end of Colorado to the other, and visited all of the state's 64 counties and practically every city and town, in order to complete the project. John also agreed to tour Colorado in 2012 and 2013 to present his photography and recount his impressions of GOCO's accomplishments, in dozens of venues across the state at events hosted by Colorado's land protection community.

John Fielder lives in Summit County, Colorado. He operates a fine art gallery, John Fielder's Colorado, in Denver's Art District on Santa Fe. He teaches photography workshops to adults and children. Information about John and his work can be found at **johnfielder.com**. Copies of all of his books and calendars, including these Great Outdoors Colorado books, can be ordered online, or by calling his gallery at 303-744-7979.